CANNON BALL!

Cannonball!

Jump in, the water is warm!

Health, Wealth, and Happiness,

12 SUCCESS PRINCIPLES
CHILDREN CAN TEACH US
ABOUT LIFE AND BUSINESS

CANNON BALL!

JAKE DIXON

LIFEWISE BOOKS

CANNONBALL!

12 SUCCESS PRINCIPLES CHILDREN CAN TEACH US ABOUT LIFE AND BUSINESS

BY JAKE DIXON

Important Note:
Nothing in this book is artificial. No artificial intelligence program was used during any stage of writing this book. The outline, chapter titles, and text were all written without the assistance of any software. This book is a passion project for me, and the work was never surrogated to a program to make it easier to complete. I willingly embrace the imperfections and long hours it took, knowing it is one hundred percent my words.

Published by:

 LIFEWISE BOOKS

PO BOX 1072
Pinehurst, TX 77362
LifeWiseBooks.com

To contact the author: Jake-Dixon.com

ISBN: 978-1-958820-54-4 (print)
ISBN: 78-1-958820-55-1 (ebook)

DEDICATION

To my wife and two daughters: You are the love of my life and have taught me so much. The wisdom and unconditional support I have received from you have inspired me to write this book, and my hope is it inspires others.

Our deepest fear is not that we are inadequate. Our deepest fear is that we are powerful beyond measure. It is our light, not our darkness that most frightens us. We ask ourselves, Who am I to be brilliant, gorgeous, talented, fabulous? Actually, who are you not to be? You are a child of God. Your playing small does not serve the world. There is nothing enlightened about shrinking so that other people won't feel insecure around you.

We are all meant to shine, as children do. We were born to make manifest the glory of God that is within us. It's not just in some of us; it's in everyone. And as we let our own light shine, we unconsciously give other people permission to do the same. As we are liberated from our own fear, our presence automatically liberates others.

MARIANNE WILLIAMSON

CONTENTS

INTRODUCTION

During the winter of 2022, our family was on a mini vacation at The Wilderness Resort in Wisconsin Dells, WI. The resort features a large indoor water park, so we spent the early part of the day splashing around and jumping through waves in the wave pool. It was filled with smiles, laughs, and priceless memories. After a few hours, we were hungry for lunch, so we took a break and talked about what everyone wanted to do next. After all, we should wait an hour before swimming again, right? No way! Our youngest daughter chimes in first and says, "Let's go on slides!" She is all about adventure, speed, and trying new things. On the other hand, our oldest daughter is exactly the opposite. She is much more reserved and timid and likes the predictable. Needless to say, fast water slides have never been her favorite because she thinks they are scary.

As parents, we were at a crossroads and proceeded to talk both into checking out the water slides. Once we arrived, our oldest daughter immediately began to freeze up and said there was no way she was going, yet our youngest was begging to go. So what were we to do? After some coaxing, I took our youngest daughter on the slide while my wife stayed with our oldest daughter, safely rooted on the ground level.

The water slide was a blast! My daughter and I immediately said to them, "It was so much fun; you have to try it!" As predicted, it was met with resistance. In my heart of hearts, I knew that if my oldest daughter would just try it, she would have a lot of fun. The hard part was getting her to try it in the first place. Like any good parent, I resorted to bribery. I promised our oldest daughter twenty dollars for a game she enjoys playing online, and she hesitantly agreed to go on the slide. Nervous, scared, and constantly second-guessing, she rode in the tube with me while screaming and laughing the entire way. When the slide finally ended, I asked her what she thought, and she raved about how much fun she had. In fact, she loved it so much she literally went on it another ten to fifteen times without me! This story encompasses the heartbeat of this book.

Growing up, I remember spending countless Midwest summer days at the local municipal pool. Without fail, I shouted "Cannonball!" like nearly every kid, as we dashed into the cool water to take a plunge. As a kid, I imagined the echo of my "warning" could be heard from miles away. In reality, the shout was likely lost in the splashing sounds around the pool, but for that brief moment, I felt invincible and unstoppable. I couldn't see the effects of my splash underwater, but when I came up for air, I knew the water must have shot up twenty feet high when I hit the water. I would always look to make sure my parents were watching as I sought out their praise and confirmation of how huge the splash was.

What is significant about the story of a kid like me doing a cannonball into a pool? Like most kids, I never thought twice about jumping in the pool. Kids rush towards the water without hesitation or fear and proceed with an all-in attitude. At that moment, the least of their concerns is how cold the water may be. It is not even a question because the reward of being in a pool far outweighs any discomfort from being cold that they may have. They greet the opportunity with a decided heart, enthusiasm, and eagerness.

As an adult, something changes. We take our time approaching the water and dip our toes in first. This same behavior follows us through other areas of life where we are a little less eager, a little less playful, and a little more hesitant to approach anything with some risk involved. We want to assess the scene and process the information first to see if the pros outweigh the cons. We dip our toes in and immediately play out the scene in our head. We begin judging. We begin asking "what if" and factoring in what others might say. *Will they call me crazy? Will I look silly? What if I mess up and embarrass myself in front of others? What if I fail?*

Where did we lose the drive to go all in and throw caution to the wind? When did we get conditioned to be timid and let fear stand in the way of just jumping in? One common lesson many leadership books have taught me is that most of us are driven by two things: pain and pleasure. We are either moving away from pain or moving towards pleasure. The reality is most of the time the avoidance of pain influences the decisions we make more so than the pursuit of what we desire.

You are reading this book right now for a reason. Whether you are a parent, an entrepreneur, or a leader, I intend to give a relatable template for success principles by utilizing stories in my own life as a parent, athlete, and business owner. Without intentional awareness, the success principles children can teach us could be missed, not to mention reflecting on the lessons we can extract from our experiences. However, for those willing to be present, intentional, and attentive, we stand to receive priceless rewards needed to be successful in our adult lives.

In many ways as adults, we have been slowly conditioned to lose sight of our own dreams, visions, and goals. We have learned to accept mediocrity and complacency and settle for average. Yet would we tell our kids to be "good enough?" Would we encourage them to grow up and be average? Would we allow them to believe that things are not possible and tell them they should just be realistic? No, of course not! So why do we tell ourselves those things? It is time to stir up that restless inner child in all of us, reconnect with our playful hearts and proceed with child-like faith.

This book can be a catalyst for your life if you allow it to be. Each chapter begins with a personal story about one of our children to emphasize a success principle. I will also share a story from my own life to further support the success principle. Following these stories will be lessons and principles we will explore together to determine how they may apply to your life as well. At the end of each chapter, you will be asked to reflect on and answer helpful questions along with an end-of-chapter exercise. This book is founded on principles that have stood the test of time. My wish is that you refer to this book often as you go through various stages of life. Go through the questions and exercises periodically throughout your journey. I am excited to share these experiences and success principles with you.

Please be sure to visit us at Jake-Dixon.com
for free downloads including the Cannonball
Workbook as well as further engagement with
Jake and the Cannonball Community.

We always love hearing from you. Be sure to share your thoughts and journey with us so we can encourage you along the way. In the wise words of Mother Teresa, "I alone cannot change the world, but I can cast a stone across the water to create many ripples."

CHAPTER 1

WHEN THE WHY IS BIG ENOUGH, THE HOW DOES NOT MATTER

*"When we know why we do what we do, everything falls into place.
When we don't, we have to push things into place."*

SIMON SINEK

YOUR WHY SHOULD MAKE YOU CRY

I once heard that your "Why" should make you cry. It is only appropriate to share the birth of our two daughters to frame this message. Henry Ward Beecher famously said, "We never know the love of a parent until we become parents ourselves." Our oldest daughter was born in 2013, and our youngest daughter was born seventeen months later. Nothing can prepare a parent for the moment when their child is born. I will never forget the nervous feeling we had and the suspense of meeting our daughters for the first time. Every emotion was experienced, leading up to these special moments. As we anxiously awaited the answers, every question was certainly asked, like, *Will the baby be healthy? What will we name her? Who is she going to resemble the most? Will I ever sleep again? How do I change a dirty diaper? Am I ready to be a parent?*

The birth of a child put life into perspective for me. Until then, it was all about *me*. I would constantly wonder what career path I wanted to pursue, how much money I would make in a year, what show I wanted to watch, what I would make for dinner, etc. However, our two daughters changed all of that. I realized it was no longer about me. My big Why changed overnight, becoming the most significant shift of priorities in my life. I quickly realized all the questions I had did not even need an answer. We would figure it out because our daughters deserved nothing but the best.

I did not need to understand how to change a diaper or whether I would ever sleep again. When the why is big enough, the how does not matter. We do what it takes to provide when the reasons *why* outweigh the reasons why *not*—having a clear why and a sense of purpose makes us superhuman. It forces us to become resourceful, creative, and solution based. We were not handed an instruction manual when our children were born, but the sense of responsibility that overtook me was so powerful that it made a lasting impact on how I approach everything. Even to this day, when I am working, I imagine our two daughters watching me on a live stream video, and I spend every moment making sure I am modeling the behavior I expect them to have when they grow up so I can make them proud.

JUST A GUY AND A BASEBALL FIELD

During the Summer of 2015, we were at a crossroads. It was clear that God was working through me, and all I had to do was listen, trust, and obey. I distinctly remember, as I was letting our dogs out one night, looking up to the sky praying God would open doors and show me the way. At the time, we had two very young children, and I had the responsibility to provide for them. We were struggling financially because I had built a large business in network marketing that quickly fell apart while also serving as the CEO of a real estate office. Although we were successful on the surface, we had been irresponsible with our money as a young married couple and put ourselves in a bind to catch up with back taxes and credit card debt.

The following week, I noticed a social media post from a fellow CEO whom I heavily admired and had heard speak on stage at large company conventions. She was seeking a CEO to assist her with a new office she had just taken over. Curious to know what the opportunity would look like, I took a shot and messaged her. I did not expect to hear back, let alone be considered a serious candidate for the role. Yet, I quickly found myself in conversations with her about moving my family to North Carolina for this new opportunity. This came as a surprise to the entire family when I shared this opportunity since I had not consulted with them before reaching out.

After much consideration, we decided to pursue this opportunity as we felt it could be the answer we were looking for and a way out of our current situation. I was presented with an offer that would position my family with significant financial gain and limitless opportunities. Knowing my wife trusted me, the decision ultimately was mine to make. One night, I drove up to a local baseball field and sat in my car for hours contemplating. The weight of the decision was substantial because I knew if it was meant to be, it was up to me. I was in tears, knowing that if I said yes to this opportunity, it would mean moving our kids away from family. I thought back to that night one week earlier when I said the prayer and could not help but smirk, thinking, *Now the big man upstairs is just showing off.*

I decided to close my eyes and speak with Him again. I put on one of my favorite songs, "I Will Praise You in This Storm" by Casting Crowns, on repeat. While the song was playing, I took out a scratch piece of paper and wrote a letter to my family. I was not sure whether I would even give it to them, but I had to get my thoughts and heart on paper as if I would. It was my promise to them, a letter of no regrets. It was placing faith over fear, knowing that neither can be seen, so I may as well choose faith. The letter represented my commitment to their future and our success as a family. I did not allow myself to dwell on the negative "what ifs." Failure was not an option, and there was no looking back. This was our shot, and it was clear that my big Why was my family, and I would do whatever it took to capitalize on this opportunity.

Saying yes in that moment led to a future we had only imagined. After multiple moves, this one decision brought more opportunities that resulted in growing our business, which has afforded us the freedom, flexibility, and financial security we had always dreamed about. I learned that when we are clear about our big Why and fully committed to doing what it takes to provide the life our family deserves, the how will take care of itself. Putting one foot in front of the other and aligning our decisions with a greater purpose has made all the difference.

LESSONS AND SUCCESS PRINCIPLES
The Big Why

Mark Twain wrote, "The two most important days in your life are the day you are born and the day you find out why." As a coach, I have worked with thousands of entrepreneurs to discover their Big Why. It can be incredibly challenging to reflect, discover, and tap into the emotion to uncover their Big Why on their own because it is often presented as an intimidating topic, causing people to freeze. Many times, an individual lacks clarity on their real purpose in life, so they end up aimlessly moving from one job to another, hoping to find fulfillment. The Big Why has been a critical component when it comes to finding purpose and fulfillment. Put simply, our Big Why is our internal motivation. It is the reason we wake up every day. The Big Why is what stirs our soul. It gets us through adversity and challenges when we step back and reconnect. When times get tough, and we feel like quitting, the Big Why can re-align us by providing the perspective we need. It is used as a tool to dig deep and continue forward because we know the Big Why is greater than ourselves. It is greater than any feeling or emotion we are experiencing at that moment. It is what gives clarity and purpose when our thoughts try to tell us the sacrifice is not worth the temporary discomfort we are experiencing. The Big Why connects us with a superior energy that gives our will the resolve it needs to forge ahead when others on the outside depend on us to keep going.

Without knowing our Big Why, we become a wandering generality instead of a meaningful specific. I remember the first time I was introduced to the concept. To be honest, initially, I thought it was some hocus pocus coming out of the mouths of people who swore by the law of attraction. I was a skeptic, stubborn, and seemingly too cool to buy into the importance of a Big Why. I was too busy pursuing status, recognition, and how much money I could make. Those vapid idols led me down a path of emptiness and irresponsibility. After the constant feeling of going through the motions and pursuing shallow rewards, I began to wake up to the teachings of many successful people I looked up to. I noticed they all had things in common, one of which was the importance they placed on identifying their Big Why.

I decided to submit to the process and did an online exercise that one of my favorite authors sold as a course. This exercise took me through self-discovery with the outcome of identifying my Big Why and being able to articulate it in one sentence. Here is what came of that day that I have saved for all these years: "To help others reach their fullest potential so they can go beyond their perspective of what they thought was possible." This was the first time I could summarize what had been stirring my soul for so many years. That simple sentence was generated after hours of going through an exercise, answering questions, and reflecting on what was most important to me. The best part is that my Why statement does not have to impress you, and yours does not need to impress me. What matters most is that it can be understood, articulated, and passionately felt every time it is read while bringing to remembrance what it is all for in the first place.

For me, the realization that others were counting on me made me take bold, decisive, and immediate action. The realization that God put me on this earth to pour into others and inspire them to be the best version of themselves became a responsibility instead of a pursuit of recognition or money. As Zig Ziglar famously said, "You can have everything in life you want if you will just help enough people get what they want." The key word there is "enough." Was I helping enough people? This question began to reveal to me that

I was playing small, and it was time to play bigger now that I had clarity around my Big Why. I realized that if it were important to me, I would find a way, and if it were not important to me, I would find an excuse.

Why Power vs. Will Power

It is fair to assume we have days that are more challenging than others, right? What is it that gets us through them? What is it that gives us the conviction to still show up? When "adulting" is hard and life throws us a curve ball, what do we have in place to either push us or, at times, pull us forward? We often say everything begins and ends with a mindset. If we do not get our heads in the game, we will be less productive, less energetic, and less effective.

Can you think of someone who is constantly negative and drains your energy when you are around them? Conversely, can you think of someone optimistic, passionate, and who inspires you? Who would you rather be around?

Ask yourself, how am I showing up? Which person am I being? Am I repelling, or am I attracting people? As we go through life, it is easy to say things like, "I'm having a bad day," when we often just had a bad five minutes. I want to introduce you to the difference between Why Power and Will Power. Both are important, and when they work together, we are unstoppable. Let's explore Will Power first.

Willpower is "the ability to control one's actions, emotions, or urges...strong determination that allows one to do something difficult."[1] It plays a vital role in our success, habits, and motivation. However, willpower can quickly be drained or easily manipulated by distractions and other outside forces. In my own life, I know willpower alone is not enough. It is too dependent on how I am feeling at any given moment. During my everyday work, I constantly witness this relationship. For example, I often speak to other real estate leaders about willpower and motivation. We constantly question, "Why do eighty-seven percent of real estate agents fail?" Many people resort to saying those agents were not motivated. They label them without ever seeking first to understand and instead, cast them aside as another statistic. I refuse to believe that. I believe every person is motivated, and God did not place someone on this earth to be average, unmotivated, or excited to fail. As leaders, we must tap into what motivates and inspires them, spend time helping them by asking tough questions, digging deep, and uncovering their Why Power.

When a person only taps into their willpower, it often shifts the focus to things such as the negative, what is difficult, or painting an unappealing picture of an activity that a person may not want to do. All these thoughts quickly drain their willpower battery. It is like a cell phone. At night, we plug in our phones to recharge because throughout the day the battery drained. We wake up the next morning with a full charge on our phones, but what happens as the day goes on? What happens if we talk on our phones a lot in the morning? What happens if we have a lot of applications running in the background? It drains our battery, and by the afternoon, the phone may shut off from usage and have no charge left to operate.

Is it enough to depend on a single power source when it comes to our lives? Is willpower, rest, exercise, and eating right enough? Or do our goals and ambitions require us to tap into a different form of energy? Perhaps one that comes from a different source, something greater than us, something from deep within, and something given to us from a higher power?

After all, when we generally speak about willpower, it can be to resist a certain temptation, to say no to something, or to muster up the courage to do something we may be dreading. If this happens at the end of the day, our energy is zapped from all these decisions that required willpower earlier in the day, and we are on empty. I don't know about you, but I do not want the ebb and flow of my feelings or mindset to always be focusing on what I do not want to do or what I cannot have. Instead, this is where Why Power comes into play.

How do we apply our Big Why in our daily lives? We know our why should make us cry, and if our why is big enough, the how does not matter. But rather than hearing these catchy quotes, have we truly accepted them into our hearts and minds? Have we dug deep to uncover *why* we do what we do? What inspires us? What is our purpose? What gives us the most energy? What is our highest and best use to impact others and ourselves? What stirs our souls and makes our hearts sing? These questions offer a different energy, don't they? It is not necessarily about *us* when it comes to Why Power. With willpower, it is one hundred percent all about us, and that is why it can be so exhausting, emotional, and difficult. However, when it comes to Why Power, it is not just about us anymore. When it is just about us, we will let ourselves down, but when others depend on us, it is hard to justify letting them down on our word.

Think of a time in your life when you were willing to let yourself down but that changed the minute someone else was depending on you. Take going to the gym, for example. I am not afraid to admit that I never enjoyed going to the gym. I was never that person to get excited at the thought of waking up early to run and lift weights. I tried using my willpower in the past because logically I knew getting up at 5:00 a.m. to work out was the right thing to do. There was no debating whether it was beneficial for my health, fitness, mindset, and energy. However, that was never enough. When the alarm clock went off, my mind immediately fought for excuses. My mind immediately argued with my body and generally won by justifying all the reasons I should not go. After all, I will do it later, right? Wrong. From 2001 to 2006, I was placed in the same scenario; except now, I had a whole college baseball team depending on me to show up at 4:30 a.m. for four consecutive years. Something changed—I was not able to focus solely on myself anymore. I knew the team was counting on me. The Big Why to show up for them was stronger than any excuse I could give myself. If I did not show up at 4:30 a.m. to the weight room, the entire team would suffer, and I was not willing to let that be the case.

Why Power taps into a different energy source that is tethered to something greater than just us. When we gain clarity and plug into our Why Power, it gives us a different charge, a bigger jolt, more enthusiasm, more purpose, and one that is available and sustainable every minute of every day. The key is having clarity since clarity is power. We must condition ourselves to tap into that Why Power throughout the day and never forget why we do what we do, not to mention who is counting on us.

For you, maybe it starts with going from success (about yourself) to significance (about others). Maybe it is about living in a state of freedom with total peace of mind financially, relationally, spiritually, and emotionally. Maybe it is about your family and building the life and legacy they deserve. Whatever it may be, the point is, when you think of your Big Why and you hear the original words you spoke, it sends a chill up your spine and produces energy that makes you act with conviction. It is being able to tap into that greater energy source on demand, forcing you to gain perspective, and immediately take constructive action.

To help uncover your Big Why, here are some questions you can ask yourself. Think and write down anything that comes to mind. It is important not to overthink but rather allow yourself to *feel*. Whatever comes to mind, write it down; do not second guess it. There will be another time you can worry about refining and condensing things down. Do not be deceived by the simplicity of the questions; they are meant to be open-ended and let you explore.

EXAMPLE EXERCISES:

1. ASK *WHY* FIVE TIMES.

Example: Let's assume you want to start running and exercising regularly to lose weight and feel great. Why? Why is this important to you? Why does it matter? A good exercise is to insert your goal and your reason into the following sentence:

_____ is important to me because

_____.

For example, *running a 5k is important to me because it will help me get into shape.*

Then, insert the reason into the first part of the sentence and repeat the process over and over again at least five times.

For example:

- Getting in shape is important to me because I don't have enough energy to be productive at work.

- Having energy at work is important to me because it's important to provide for my family.

- Providing for my family is important to me because being a great parent is rewarding.

- Being a great parent is important to me because I believe it's part of leading a good life.

- Leading a good life is important to me because I want to know my life mattered and made an impact on others.

Now we are getting somewhere. Suddenly, your goal of running a race is not just about getting into shape. It is about progressing in your career, providing for your family, and living a life you are proud of. Get beneath the surface. Keep asking why. Why does this matter? Why is this important? Why now? The deeper you dig, the more you will learn about yourself and about what matters to you.

2. WHAT GETS YOU OUT OF BED IN THE MORNING, AND WHAT KEEPS YOU UP AT NIGHT? WHAT EXCITES YOU?

Focusing on what excites you is great life advice in general. If you are not excited about what you are doing, it is going to be hard to stick with it. Eventually, your enthusiasm will fade, your motivation will disappear, and your willpower will run out. Instead of focusing on things you *think* you should do this year, ask yourself, what do you *desire* to do? What would you be excited about doing? What is going to be fun and bring you joy? Maybe, instead of a new gym membership, it is enrolling in a dance class, or it is running on trails to enjoy the beauty of the outdoors, instead of treadmills. Whatever it is, make it something that excites you. By doing so, you won't be relying solely on willpower or motivation.

3. WHAT SENTENCE WILL COME TO DEFINE YOUR LIFE?

Most people want to do it all. At times, our hopes and dreams have no limits. The challenge with wanting to do it all is that you end up lacking focus and fail to set priorities. When is a time in your life when you accomplished something you are proud of? Think back to it and consider if you were focused on accomplishing it or allowed distractions or side projects to derail you. I bet you were laser-focused.

Think about what you want your life-defining sentence to be. How would you like to be remembered? Maybe it is about raising great kids or volunteering for a cause you care deeply about. Maybe it is being an artist who creates beautiful things that make people's lives a little more enjoyable. Maybe it is starting a thriving business that solves a pressing challenge. To write a great sentence, you will need energy, focus, and optimism. You will need to maintain good mental and physical health. You will need to be active and surround yourself with other ambitious people who inspire and give you energy.

4. WHAT WILL PEOPLE SAY AT YOUR 80TH BIRTHDAY PARTY?

This is a common personal development exercise because it helps you put your life into perspective and figure out what you want to accomplish and how you want to be remembered. Imagine your 80th birthday party. Who is attending? What are you doing at this celebration? What have you accomplished? Create a picture of what you want this to look like. Are you still in good physical health? Have you lived a life of action, determined to set goals, and achieve them? Did you live life to the fullest and capitalize on opportunities that came your way? Did you relentlessly pursue passion and purpose?

Most likely, you will want these answers to be a resounding YES, and be able to say that for eight full decades, you lived a life you were proud of and others were inspired by. You made the most of every day, accomplishing big things without regret. Take a snapshot of that mental picture. Remember the feeling and use it as fuel. It's not just going to happen. You will not magically wake up on your 80th birthday having accomplished all these things. Achieving that vision will require years of hard work, dedication, and persistence. It is on you to make it happen. In the wise words of Simon Sinek from his book *Start With Why:*[2] "People don't buy what you do, they buy WHY you do it." He also says, "Great leaders are in pursuit of why. They hold themselves accountable to how they do it, and what they do serves as the tangible proof of what they believe."

Newton's Third Law

"For every action in nature there is an equal and opposite reaction."

ISAAC NEWTON

This is a law I would commonly reference when giving baseball lessons to young kids as an example to illustrate body movements and various actions when hitting and pitching. One way to demonstrate this was by holding up my arm and flexing my bicep muscle. I would proceed to show the kids that when I flex my bicep muscle, my tricep muscle must relax. After all, for every action, there is an equal and opposite reaction. This illustration really drove the point home. This law can serve us regarding our Big Why as well. What I have found to be true is when we are clear about our Big Why, it makes decision making easier. For me personally, I have a behavior style that can lend itself to appeasing others. I can be tempted to say yes to others and put myself on the back burner, which only leads to frustration, resentment, and burnout. By getting clear on my Big Why, it helps me understand what takes priority in my life and, ultimately what I should be saying yes or no to.

I have learned to apply Newton's law to a decision-making system. Just like my previous illustration, when I say yes to something, then that means I'm saying no to something else. I have learned to calculate my response by accounting for this effect. The first step is to answer the basic question, given the scenario in front of me, what would I be saying yes and no to? Doing so pulls me into the present and creates a level of awareness I need so I do not go back to my default settings of always trying to appease others. From there, the next important question focuses on the no response. Whatever I am saying no to, am I okay with that?

Let's take a common example of eating dinner at night with the family. Imagine sitting down for a nice meal after a long day at work to finally relax, decompress, and hear about everyone else's day. You have looked forward to this time with your family because it allows you to refuel and recenter yourself. After all, much of the reason you work so hard and make the sacrifices you do is for them in the first place. Suddenly, your phone rings in the middle of dinner, and it is a call from the client you have been praying for. The voice inside your head leads with the fear of loss and asks, "What if I don't answer this call? What if I miss the sale?" At this exact moment, you have a choice to make. You can say yes to answering the phone call, or you can say no and get back to eating dinner with your family. Assume for a moment you excuse yourself from the dinner table with an innocent gesture to your family by holding up one finger, letting them know it will only take a second and proceed to take the call. The client insists you come right away because they are ready to ink the deal. Now, what do you do?

Putting judgment aside in this example, let's say you took the call and explained to your family that you must leave to get the deal put together. What just happened? Arguably, you just said yes to a deal and no to your family. Are you okay with that? Perhaps this is extreme, but is it? This happens too often and stems from a lack of clarity on the Big Why. It is one thing if the family's expectations are set and another when it becomes a trend. Things can quickly spiral out of control. The very people you work so hard to support are left to finish the evening without you. You come back to them asleep in their beds while you reheat your dinner and eat it alone. When your actions align with your Big Why, making decisions and life can become much easier. Without Big Why clarity, actions are misaligned, which can lead to resentment, burnout, and a loss of connection.

One of the most significant reasons for knowing your Big Why and tapping into that energy source is knowing when to be fully present. Allow yourself permission to say no to the good things so you can say yes to the great things. This is not an overstatement. When I gained clarity and conviction to stand for my Big Why, it saved my marriage. I was the person in the story mentioned above. I was the guy who would lay awake in bed until 2:00 a.m., working until I passed out only to look over at my wife and kids with a glance of acknowledgment that they were there. At one point, I remember my wife saying out of love that she did not have a husband anymore; she had a roommate. That shook me to the core and forced me to realign and take inventory of my choices. I had gotten so far off course and away from my Big Why, that it was the reality check I needed to make immediate changes.

I did not want my legacy to be that I was not a present husband or father. I did not want my family to grow resentful of the work I was doing. Something had to change, and it all started with me no longer bringing my laptop home from work. I removed that temptation, and it forced me to be fully present at home. No longer did work get the best of me and my family got the rest of me. After all, they were my Big Why and deserved the best of me. I once heard someone explain the difference between legacy and inheritance. It was something to the effect of legacy is the intellectual property we leave inside of others, whereas inheritance is all the material things we leave behind for others. Both certainly have their place, but one is of sentimental value, and the other is a value that will far outlast you for generations. Never forget, saying yes to something means you are saying no to something else. What is it? And are you okay with it?

QUESTIONS TO CONSIDER:

1. What stirs my soul and makes my heart sing?

2. What is my driving motivation?

3. What core values do I hold closest?

4. What will achieving my goals do for me? For others?

5. In what ways will my life change?

6. What could get in the way of accomplishing my Big Why?

7. How can I prevent that?

8. How will I overcome those challenges when they show up?

9. What do I want others to say about me?

10. What impact do I wish to have?

STOP AND COMPLETE:

Letters to Your Family: Write two letters as if you were one year into the future. The first letter (Success Letter) should describe in specific detail the feelings, emotions, and the way life looks when you accomplish your goals. The second letter (Apology Letter) should describe in specific detail the feelings, emotions, and the way life looks if you do not achieve your goals. Take your time, be precise, and allow yourself to go to that place to feel what it would be like in both scenarios. Complete this exercise in the Chapter 1 section of the Cannonball Workbook.

CHAPTER 2

WHAT DO ASTRONAUTS, OLYMPIANS, AND HORSE TRAINERS HAVE IN COMMON?

"A person without a dream has never had a dream come true."

ANDY ANDREWS

WHAT I WANT TO BE WHEN I GROW UP

On the first day of school each year, my wife has our children write on a small chalkboard what they want to be when they grow up. It is one of the most anticipated events of the year because it evolves and is generally filled with the most random surprises. For our oldest daughter, it has spanned from jobs such as horse trainer, graphic designer, animal grooming business owner, and YouTuber. For our youngest daughter, it has included things such as the owner of an animal sanctuary, animal police officer, animal rescuer, veterinarian, and professional gymnast. Regardless of the vision they have for themselves, I cannot help but stop and take in that moment every year. It gives me a glimpse into their passions, aspirations, creative imagination, and where their interests currently lie. Without fail, it takes me back to my childhood when I dreamed of being a Major League Baseball (MLB) player.

It also gives me pause every year to reflect on how many dreams, goals, and aspirations never manifested into reality. For many, something happens during their journey from childhood to adulthood. How many people grew up dreaming of being an astronaut, Olympic athlete, teacher, professional athlete, or the next president of the United States? Unfortunately, many of us growing up became conditioned to hearing "no" or phrases like, "You do not need that." This caused many dreams to slowly fade. We were told to be realistic. We adopted beliefs that we were not worthy or deserving of that level of success. We stopped asking for things we desired. Over time, we ended up setting aside our big ambitions and settling for average. I am thankful for this constant reminder and annual opportunity to slow down and reflect. Inside each of us is that young child with big goals and dreams. Sometimes we need to slow life down, extract that same creative imagination, and move with childlike faith toward what we truly want.

NONE OF YOU WILL EVER SEE THIS

My sophomore year of high school presented a defining moment for me. I grew up in a small town of seven hundred people in the middle of nowhere Illinois. We had no traffic lights or restaurants, just a rural farm town with a lot of hardworking people. Our high school had two hundred kids total with fifty being in my graduating class. I share this because I was a dreamer. I loved baseball and had goals of becoming a pro. I was an athletic kid who played multiple sports and I am six feet six inches tall, but back then, I was only 180 pounds soaking wet. Few athletes from our high school went on to play in college, let alone professionally. Generally, most kids stayed around the area and farmed. Even though many of my friends and family were involved in farming, it was not the vision I had for my future, and my heart was set on playing baseball at the most competitive levels possible.

During the second inning of a playoff baseball game, a Midwest thunderstorm moved in with heavy rain, lightning, and thunder. The umpires ended up calling off the game, and we had to postpone it until another day to finish. While the players were scrambling to pick up the equipment, our coach yelled at us to hurry up and get it inside. We were to meet him inside the gym, but apparently, we were not getting the equipment picked up quickly enough because he became more and more angry. As young athletes, I am sure we were probably goofing off to an extent and not realizing how upset he was getting. When we were inside, he sat us down and began to yell and scream, letting us know he was disappointed with us. And then it happened. He stepped toward me and put his finger within inches of my face. In front of my entire team, he proceeded to look me in the eye and said with his raised voice, "None of you will ever see the inside of a college or professional stadium unless you buy a ticket!"

Silence. I was in disbelief at what he just said, especially in front of all my teammates during a fit of rage. After all, wasn't this supposed to be my coach? Wasn't he supposed to be one of the biggest champions in my corner to encourage me to become my best? It was after that moment that I had some reflecting to do and decisions to make. I could think to myself, *Maybe he was right. Who am I to go on and play baseball in college, let alone professionally?* After all, no one had accomplished that. Thoughts raced through my head, and I began to question if he had a point. I was from a very small school, so how would any scouts find me anyway? On the other hand, I could choose the other path of defiance, one where I was not going to let him dictate what I could or could not do. I realized that just because he gave up on his goals, it did not give him permission to try and talk me out of mine. From that day forward, I committed myself to do everything in my power to prove him wrong. I stopped playing all other sports, which was not exactly a popular decision in a small town when you are six foot six inches tall and can shoot a basketball well, run, and jump.

I dedicated myself to a singular focus of working my butt off so I never could question what was possible. I decided to play to win instead of playing not to lose. I decided to use his words as fuel for motivation. I placed that chip on my shoulder and used it as inspiration every day to show myself and others what was possible. I went on to play college and professional baseball. I am proud to say I went on to see some amazing stadiums and had the best view, standing on that pitching mound and playing in front of thousands of people.

The story did not end there. I realized later in life that the real gift in that moment was not the ability to prove him or anyone else wrong. The real gift he gave me that day was lighting an eternal flame inside of me that is unapologetic, fierce, and committed to never being that person toward someone else. It made me who I am today by having an intense passion and belief to succeed that I can pour into others. I will never be that person who says you cannot do something. No one can measure a committed heart, but you can see it in the other person's eyes when they have it. Life did not happen *to* me after that game; life happened *for* me. Our environment or the opinions of others do not dictate what we can achieve. It is the will, determination, and hunger inside of us that does.

LESSONS AND SUCCESS PRINCIPLES
Priority Management

Whether it be living vicariously through my kids on what they desire to be when they grow up or examples from my own life when someone tells me I cannot do something, one of the common lessons I have been able to extract is the ability to prioritize what is most important, or keeping the main thing the main thing as Stephen Covey, the author of *Seven Habits of Highly Effective People,*[3] writes.

Philosopher Lewis Gordon is quoted as saying, "There is nothing more powerful than the made-up mind." The ability for us to identify what is most important and then relentlessly pursue it is critical to success. I have coached thousands of business owners, and when I ask them to define their goals, it is generally vague. They want to lose weight. They want to make more money. It is not specific because, often, they lack a sense of clarity on what is most important. I can sense hesitation on their part when setting a clear goal because it begs the question, "What's next?" and "What do I need to prioritize?". Stepping out and being exposed like that is uncomfortable to many. They realize they can no longer hide. Once they hear themselves define the goals, followed by the priorities to achieve them, there is no turning back.

A lot of people will blame time. They claim they do not have enough time to accomplish their goals, so they end up retreating into a world of mediocrity. How is it that high achievers can accomplish things that many others dream of when they have the same number of hours in a day? How can Elon Musk build rockets that travel into outer space? How is it that Helen Keller was deaf and blind yet graduated cum laude and did so much for women's suffrage and labor rights? How is it that Harriet Tubman escaped slavery and then underwent thirteen missions to rescue approximately seventy enslaved people, including her family and friends, using the network of antislavery activists and safe houses known collectively as the Underground Railroad?

Amazing accomplishments are all around us, filled with stories of ordinary people doing extraordinary things. Many had bigger hurdles to overcome than you and I can imagine, yet they did not let the excuse of time or lack of clarity prevent them from accomplishing their goals. The common DNA all high achievers share is a keen awareness of priorities. They can cut through the noise and have a singular focus on the desired outcome. If you ask most adults, "How are you doing?" they will respond with something related to time. They may say things like, "Good, I am just so busy!". It is the default response many people use to justify their lack of action. Through coaching, I have observed that many people will artificially manufacture problems, making things appear more complicated. Then, they hide behind that complexity as justification for future failures or inactions.

Our ability to eliminate excuses and stop making lack of achievement about time deficiency is critical to our success. Time is the most precious currency available to us. We all have an equal amount of time in the day. No one gets any bonus minutes for doing good deeds. Look at it this way, time is the great equalizer. We cannot manage time; it is going to be continuous, no matter how hard we try to stop it. Many people question how they should "spend" their time as if it is dollars and cents, yet never slow down to calculate the real cost. I believe we do not spend time, and we cannot manage time. We simply utilize time, and the choice is ours on how we do it.

By narrowing the focus and doubling down on our priorities, it becomes a magnifying glass. Similar to a young child who uses a magnifying glass in the sun, it creates a beam of light so hot it can set the tinder on fire. The same is true for us and our daily actions. When we are clear about what we want, why we want it, and focus our actions to achieve it, that becomes the magnifying glass to light our ambitions on fire. The fun part is that when the fire is lit, our light will shine for many to see, and others will come from miles away to sit around and feel the warmth. We owe ourselves and others to have the discipline and focus to establish our priorities so that our light can shine and illuminate the world.

How do we establish priorities then? For many, this can be challenging, but it can be simpler than we think. Let's start with what *not* to do. When we use time and busyness as the excuse, it is generally a self-fulfilling prophecy. Let's face it, most people like lists. Magazines, online articles, and YouTube videos are created to appeal to lists. "The Top Five Ways to Lose Weight" or "The Eleven Steps to Become Successful." We love to see things broken down into steps because our brains can process information more easily. I am a fan of lists, yet when was the last time we stopped to analyze the quality of the list itself and whether it serves or works against us? Take a to-do list, for example. We can have a to-do list that goes on for days. When we create a to-do list, it instantly creates a sense of overwhelm to the point of getting paralyzed; therefore, we take no action at all. The reality is that there is never enough time in the day to do everything, and yet there is always enough time to do the most important things.

Instead of operating from a to-do list, what if we narrowed the focus down? What if we took a magnifying glass to our list? A success tip is creating a to-do, should-do, and must-do list. Out of the list of items we wish to accomplish, what items need to be on each list? This forces us to acknowledge that not all items are weighted equally, so we can begin to pull some out to highlight. However, that is not enough. We often joke that many people "should" all over themselves, so the next step is to examine our should-do list and break it down even further into our must-do list. The must-do items carry the greatest importance and must be done before anything else. When we can identify our must-do items, we have successfully prioritized our time. We may end up with three to five items rather than the original fifty we started with. Consider asking, "If I do nothing else today other than _____, I will consider it a successful day." Focusing questions like this can work magic when learning priority management.

Questions to Ask:

1. What do I really want?

2. What is most important to me?

3. What do I value the most?

4. How can I make the greatest impact?

5. What is the one thing I can do that would make everything else easier or unnecessary?

6. What are my must-dos for today compared to my to-dos?

7. If I did nothing else today, what should consume the greatest amount of my energy and focus?

Another great tip is creating a filtration system for your ideas and actions to flow through. If we can build guard rails around our lives, they can help us fend off distractions, so we can prioritize what gets our attention. Wouldn't that be helpful? Any time we do something two or more times, we should create a system for it. Needless to say, we will find ourselves sorting through activities daily, so creating a system for how to filter what is important and urgent versus what is not important and not urgent can help determine our priorities.

A common system to help with this is called the Eisenhower Matrix, developed by former President Dwight D. Eisenhower. The Eisenhower Matrix is a task management tool that helps us organize and prioritize tasks by urgency and importance. It begins with making a quadrant on a piece of paper. Above the top left quadrant is marked "Urgent." Next to the top left quadrant is "Important." Above the top right quadrant is marked "Not Urgent." And the bottom left quadrant has "Less Important" next to it. See the example here:

The Eisenhower Matrix

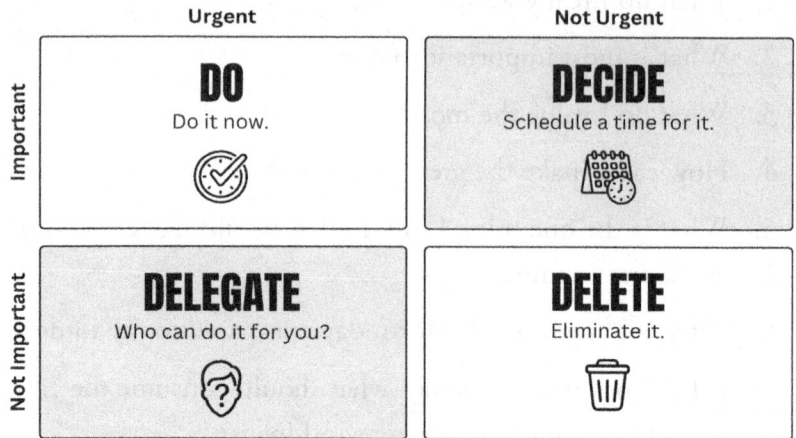

The filtration system works like this:

1. Anything in the top left quadrant that is urgent and important should be done first.

2. Anything in the top right quadrant that is not urgent but is important should be scheduled out and completed by you at a future time.

3. Anything in the bottom left quadrant that is urgent but not important for you to do can be delegated to someone else.

4. Anything in the bottom right quadrant that is not urgent and not important for you to do can simply be eliminated.

Next time there is a massive list of items that need to be done, try placing the specific items in the Eisenhower Matrix and see how many are in the urgent and important quadrant compared to how many are not. This single exercise can be the key to unlocking priorities and seizing goals and ambitions.

Be the Farmer of Your Mind

> "Whether you think you can, or you
> think you can't—you're right."
>
> **HENRY FORD**

I remember listening to an amazing audiobook of the late Earl Nightingale called *The Strangest Secret.*[4] In this book, Nightingale says, "Whatever we plant in our subconscious mind and nourish with repetition and emotion will one day become reality. We are all self-made, but only the successful will admit it." Dreaming big and setting goals all start with a mindset. Our mind is a powerful tool if we know how to properly use it. I decided to adopt Nightingale's philosophy and give it a try years ago. The part that stood out to me most was what he said about repetition (frequency) and emotion (intensity). In essence, couldn't the same argument be made in relationship to our memories? Aren't memories just the experiences we have had and the emotional intensity we give them?

As far back as I can remember, I have dreamt of having a house on a lake in the mountains. There was just something about the calm I would feel every time I was near water. I remember going through some hardships in college and my default setting was to go sit by the lake to journal, think, and reflect. I remember watching shows on television and admiring the lakefront houses others were able to own. I took this idea to social media by posting pictures of houses each year and publicly stating one day I would have that dream home on a lake. Out of all the posts I made, one stood out the most. Back in 2012, I posted saying that in three years I would own my dream home on a lake. I remember at that time I was speaking differently and with more conviction because enough was enough. I could continue to wish it into existence, or I could finally make it happen.

In 2015, my family and I moved to Wisconsin, and my only requirement was to buy a dream home on a lake within the rustic scenery of the Wisconsin bluffs surrounded by beautiful trees in the area. To me, this was my chance to make it happen once and for all. We purchased and closed on our dream home in the summer of 2015. Little did I remember that on the exact day of our closing, three years prior, I posted declaring that within three years, we would be in our lakefront home. Let me repeat: on the same day we closed on the home, my social media memories reminded me of what I had posted three years prior! Coincidence? I think not.

When we dream big and grant ourselves permission to assign an emotional intensity to it, our conscious and sub-conscious mind will get to work to turn dreams into reality. I would obsess about owning a home on the lake. I would literally have dreams about it. Every time I closed my eyes and pictured an amazing future for our children, it always involved a home on a lake in this exact setting. As Nightingale essentially said, we become what we think about all the time, and the frequency and intensity of what we feed our minds end up turning into reality.

What are we allowing into our minds? My friend and mentor, Nick, coined the phrase "chief marketing officer of my mind." We are constantly bombarded with billions of dollars' worth of ads because the companies are competing for our attention. They want to win the mind-share battle. Are we acting as the chief marketing officer of our mind? Just as a farmer plants seeds in the field, we get to plant what goes into our minds. Farmers work tirelessly in the fields and make sure they are planting the correct crop for the upcoming season. After the crop is planted, they constantly tend to the field with fertilizer and water, so the plants grow into a healthy and full crop. When the crop is mature and ready to be harvested, the farmer heads out to reap.

This is exactly how our minds work. As Robert Louis Stevenson wrote, "Don't judge each day by the harvest you reap but by the seeds that you plant." Our mind does not know if the seeds we are planting are healthy or toxic. If we plant the wrong seed and continue to water it with frequency and intensity, we will reap what we sow. Similarly, if we plant the right seed and continue to water it with frequency and intensity, then we will stand to harvest the bountiful fruits of that labor.

One of our daughters came home with an exercise she did that was stuffed in her school folder. My wife pulled it out and could not wait to show me. The exercise was the silhouette of a person's head, and the kids were asked to fill in the white space by answering the question, "What is on your mind today?" They were instructed to fill their heads with words, drawings, and images to represent what they were thinking and feeling. I was stopped right in my tracks. I could not believe our nine-year-old daughter was filling in this space with some of the most beautiful words I have ever read.

"Be nice to others."
"Always try your best."
"Be nice no matter what."
"Never give up on yourself."
"Don't quit."
"Nothing is impossible."
"To never give up on your dreams."

"Something is always possible."

"My personality."

"How I am different."

"Puppies."

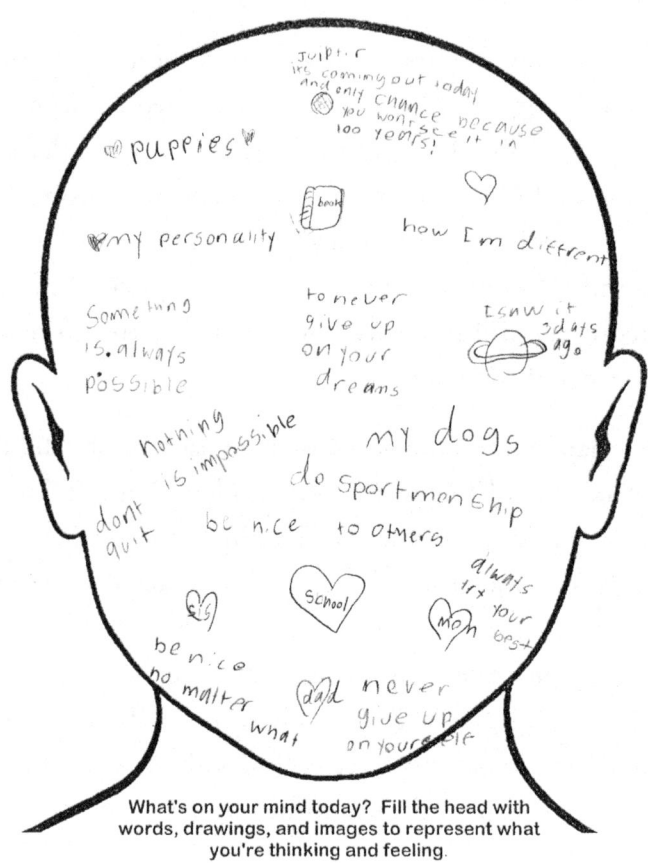

What's on your mind today? Fill the head with
words, drawings, and images to represent what
you're thinking and feeling.

As you can see in the image, these are just some of the things she wrote down that day. I will make many mistakes in my life, but if I get anything right, it is being a strong father who instilled this type of mindset into our daughters. The most important conversation we have in a day is the one that we have in our own minds. Furthermore, it is said in leadership trainings I have attended that people grow into the conversations they create around them. If we combine the two concepts, doesn't it stand to reason that the most important conversation we have in a day is the one in our minds, which means we are growing into the conversation we are having with ourselves? When we protect our thoughts, we, in turn, are the chief marketing officers of our minds and take a stand for our authentic success.

It's key for us to pay attention to what seeds we are planting in our minds. Are we watering them frequently or just planting them and moving on? We must protect our minds from the poison others may try to plant in them. Yes, there will be skeptics and haters. Yes, we will be tested. But if we continue to plant well, water, and cultivate those seeds frequently, while applying an emotional intensity to them, then our big dreams will manifest into reality when combined with the right priorities and actions that matter most.

The Importance of Setting Goals

Think back to the last time you went grocery shopping. How much preparation went into it before you left home? For most, it involves sitting down at the kitchen table and focusing on what is needed for the week. It may involve getting up and taking inventory of what is on hand, skimming through recipes, and looking at what is on the family calendar each night. Either way, it took planning and preparation. What about your last vacation? How much preparation went into it before you left for a week of fun? For most, it involved a lot of research. Perhaps you spoke to friends who went to the same destination. Maybe you went to research things online or even watched videos on YouTube. From there, maybe you planned out the entire itinerary of where to stay, how long, excursions, fun places to visit, activities, and restaurants you wanted to try. Either way, it took planning and preparation.

If planning and preparation are needed for things like grocery shopping and vacation planning, then wouldn't the same be true for goal setting? After all, isn't the pursuit and accomplishment of our goals generally what funds the ability to buy groceries and go on vacations?

Logically, we can see the importance of this, and yet, after coaching numerous industry professionals, it is all too common to see the lack of planning and preparation people give to goal setting. They generally muster up a vague idea of what their goals are and have no clear plan of action to support how they are going to achieve them. My observation comes from a place not of judgment but rather of empathy. It can be painful to see adults struggle so much with identifying what they want, why they want it, and how they are going to get it, especially when I know each of them was once that child who was willing to dream without limits and answer the same questions my daughters do. For most, they are living life as a dress rehearsal and going through the motions. They do not love what they do and have settled for a life of complacency and contentment, working for a paycheck to pay bills. I refuse to believe life is about working to pay the bills. Legendary entrepreneur, author, and motivational speaker Jim Rohn put it best when he said, "We all have two choices; we can make a living or we can design a life."

Deep down I believe we all want a life by design, even though it looks different for each person. We were all born with a blank canvas and the ability to make decisions, but somewhere along the way, we handed over the paint brush to other voices and opinions and lost sight of what we truly wanted. If this is you, there is good news. You can change right now. C.S. Lewis said, "You are never too old to set a new goal or to dream a new dream." I firmly believe the restless spirit inside you and that playful spirit of the child within you are kicking and screaming to be free. You were meant to be great and find joy and fulfilment in what you do.

One of the best ways to unleash that thirst for more inside of you is with two simple words, "what if." My business today began with me asking, "What if...?" The inspiration for my writing this book originated by asking, "What if...?" If we are willing to sit in silence and ask ourselves the same question, we may be surprised what answers reveal themselves. Instead of thinking of all the reasons we shouldn't or all the reasons why it would not work, drown out the noise and ask, "What if it did work?" "What if everything went right and I could achieve it?" "What if by simply taking action, the right people who could help guide me did show up?" Starting questions with "what if" expands our thinking. It brings us into a world of possibilities. It forces us to think, dream, and wonder again like we did when we were young. Suddenly, our playful spirit comes alive, and we begin to dream again. We begin to sell ourselves on why we deserve it. We begin to find evidence around us that supports things being possible, and if others can do it, so can we. It all begins with simply asking, "What if?"

I must caution you that these "what if" type questions can be constructive or destructive. For example, if we are not careful, "what if" can lead us down the road of hesitation, worry, fear, and skepticism with thoughts like, *What if something goes wrong? What if I fail? What if they tell me no?* On the other hand, "what if" questions can be unbelievably empowering, like, *What if I knew I could not fail? What if I succeed? What if I took action and new doors of opportunity opened up to me?* Be sure to leverage the positive energy of "what if" questions and focus on all the possibilities of what could go right by you pursuing your goals.

Be S.M.A.R.T. About Your Goals

Imagine you wake up on January 1 of the new year, inspired by all the new opportunities and fresh starts the new year provides. At that moment, you declare this is a new year, so you will become a better version of yourself. This is *your* year to lose weight and get in the best shape of your life. For the first two weeks, you bought all the right foods, ate right, purchased a new gym membership, and even bought yourself some new workout clothes. Around week three, life threw you a curve ball, setting your perfect trajectory off course. Next thing you know, you were at the drive-through window, having not been to the gym for several days. Just as you were getting into a routine and overcoming soreness, life happened. Day by day, you woke up with the best intentions, and yet, the noise from the outside began to drown out the noise from within. Health and fitness plans returned to the backburner as you convinced yourself once again you would get to it later. You tried starting over again the next week, but the cycle continued from there. Does this sound familiar?

If so, it is likely due to the initial mistake many people make of not setting clear goals with specific outcomes and deadlines. As my college baseball coach would always say, "Proper preparation prevents poor performance." In a future chapter, we will outline how to create measurable action items, introduce accountability, and create a ninety-day action plan. Right now, I'd like to give you a simple acronym that has helped many high achievers set goals. The S.M.A.R.T. acronym is widely known, yet I do not want to take it for granted because what is easy to do is also easy not to do. The acronym represents:

S = Specific
M = Measurable
A = Attainable
R = Relevant
T = Time Stamped

Using this method will help you set goals that work for you rather than setting yourself up for disappointment. Saying, "I want to lose weight and get in shape," is what many people say. They fear specificity because they do not want to set themselves up for failure. Leaders will say things like, "If your dreams do not scare you, then they are not big enough." In the same way, if your goals are not specific enough, that should scare you. It is easy to state your intentions, but when you are forced to drill down into the details, you become emotionally connected to the outcome and instantly accountable.

Imagine the teams who enter the NCAA March Madness® tournament each year. Every team goes into it with the same goal—to win the championship. This means they must focus on the next game and make that the priority. To win the next game, the coach and players create a game plan. They study films of their opponents as well as themselves. They go into the game with every intention of winning and executing the plan. Throughout the game, the coaches and players must identify the measurables and know how much time is left on the clock at all times. They will constantly look up at the scoreboard to see how many fouls they have, who has possession of the ball for the next jump ball, how many time-outs they have left, what the score is, and how much time is left on the clock. By understanding the leading and lagging measures of the game, they can make real-time adjustments. Most games are won or lost in the second half. Any good coach can enter the game with a game plan, but the great coaches adjust during halftime and execute a winning strategy during the second half.

This illustrates one way that S.M.A.R.T. goals can be applied. Being specific forces you to get clear on what exactly you desire to achieve. My business coach always reminds me that clear is kind, and unclear is unkind. We must be kind to ourselves and our future selves. Clarity is power, so when we get specific about exactly what we want, we can no longer hide behind vague commitments and are forced to take a stance for our greatness more than we are willing to defend our limitations. In the March Madness example, the specific goal of winning a championship allows the entire team to rally behind a common purpose. The specific goal takes it from being an individual effort to a team effort because all involved care deeply about the result.

Once we are specific with our desired goal, how will we know whether we have accomplished it? In Major League Baseball, they keep score along with every statistic one can imagine. In t-ball, they do not keep score, and every player gets to bat. Anything measured can be improved upon. Keeping score matters. What is our score? Unfortunately, when it comes to our goals in life, there are no participation trophies. We must be clear about what we want and identify the measurables that let us know if we are on track or not. During the March Madness game, the measurables can show up in many different forms depending on the strategy of the coach. Is the measurable to get the other team's best player in foul trouble? Is the measurable to dominate the time of possession to slow the game down and keep the ball out of the other team's hands? Is the measurable to get our best player a certain number of shots in the game? Is the measurable simply whether we are winning?

Determining if our goal is attainable boils down to asking, is it genuinely possible to achieve the outcome? For example, I can say I want to make a million dollars today, and arguably, it checks off some of the S.M.A.R.T. goal boxes; however, when it comes to attainability, it forces me to pause. To be attainable, I like to take a different approach than some. I am very careful with how I explain this because I never want to determine what is realistic for someone else. I refuse to let my limiting beliefs influence your beliefs. Personally, I view whether something is attainable or not based on my deep-seated belief. Do I *truly* believe I can accomplish this? Do I have a committed heart? Do I feel it in my soul? I do not necessarily gauge attainability on whether I have personally accomplished it in the past or if someone else has. After all, everything is impossible until someone does it. I use attainability as a checkpoint for me to assess my heart and commitment to the goal. If I do not have an unwavering belief that the goal will be accomplished, it forces me to ask more questions or possibly adjust the goal. In the case of the March Madness tournament, a number sixteen seed who is about to play the number one seed in the tournament can say they have the same goal, which is to win. My argument is the team that has the most belief and in their heart knows the goal is attainable will come out victorious.

Relevancy matters when it comes to setting S.M.A.R.T. goals. The goal we set for ourselves must align with our overall objectives, core values, and beliefs. If I set out to lose twenty pounds and run a 5k this year, but my actions do not match my words, is the goal even relevant? I may have stated my desired outcome, yet all my time is spent deflecting and doing everything but working out, eating right, and getting in shape. This would be like a team in the March Madness tournament saying they want to win the championship but show up late to practice, skip warm-ups, and walk around on the court rather than engage the opponents. Relevancy matters because success is not simultaneous; it is sequential. Like dominos, we must line things up so all actions and attitudes are congruent and relevant to the desired outcome.

Finally, our goals must be time-stamped. We can set a goal by saying we want to lose twenty pounds, but it takes on a different tone when we say we want to lose them by July 27 of this year so we can go on our dream vacation and be confident in our appearance. When we cement our commitment by including a date, it allows us to compress time. All work will fill the space that time allows. Thinking back to school days, teachers assigned us a research paper that was due in three weeks. Most of us may not want to admit it, but we became experts in procrastination years ago. We started out by thinking we had plenty of time to get this done so we put it off and found other more interesting things to fill our time. The next thing we knew, the research paper we put off was then due in three days, so we stressed, built anxiety, and experienced frustration all because we put something off that had a pre-determined end date. We did not use the time leading up to the date wisely and created self-inflicted pain by procrastinating. Our goals are no different. Time is going to pass anyway, so why don't we do something every day that brings us one step closer to our desired outcome? Having a time stamp creates a useful sense of urgency and builds a heightened level of awareness. It fosters an environment of focus and productivity because there is no time to waste. Every moment counts.

How to Effectively Set Goals

Every new year, I do this exercise, and each time I isolate myself so I can focus and reflect without distraction. Since 2007, I have written a letter to myself and included highlights from the previous year and my goals for the upcoming year. I include real-world information such as where the stock market is at, what gas prices are, and what world events occurred, among other things, so that it serves as a time capsule. This exercise has evolved over the years, specifically when I was introduced to a mentor of mine in 2013.

Throughout my career, I have experienced countless leaders telling others to set goals. They bark orders and act as if the other person should know what to do. I have realized that no one has taught us how to effectively set goals. Many jump to the conclusion that people should inherently know how to set goals, and when they don't, it results in frustration or accusations of being unmotivated. Even if the individual did set proper goals for themselves, I have experienced a leader making me feel inadequate because my goals were not big enough. They said, "Now take your goal and double it." I thought to myself, wait a minute, this was my goal, and now you just told me it was not good enough, and it just became your goal. My DNA was all over my desired outcome because I was the author of it.

To assist you with identifying goals for yourself, I would like to offer you the formula I use and have taught to thousands of others ever since my mentor shared it with me. The first part is to reflect on the previous year using three key steps:

PART ONE—REFLECTING ON LAST YEAR

1. **Step One**—Complete a year in review. (Hint: This should be fun.) It's going to be on the very first page of the journal when you open it up. Simply write at the top of the page, "The Best of ____(Year)." Write down all twelve months of the year. Allow yourself space and utilize multiple pages in your journal because you will be asked to make a list of things underneath each month when they happened. Then, you will spend time writing down all the memorable experiences, accomplishments, events, and highlights you had each month. In each month, document what was the best for each month in the previous year. Did you go on a vacation? Was there a "first" experience you had? Did you receive an award or recognition? Did you have a breakthrough or achieve a milestone? There could be one or two in a month, or there could be more than ten. You are working through your journal to document the year in review and create a highlight reel of all the things you want to remember.

Pause for a moment. Imagine looking back ten years down the road, and the first page you flip to in that journal is the "Best of." You can have fun by reflecting on what you accomplished and experienced. For clarification, this initial step is not to isolate the goals you accomplished per se; it is simply to look back at the moments in time that were the most memorable and you felt were special. This is to serve as a database of memories for yourself, your children, or maybe even your grandchildren.

2. **Step Two**—Complete the learn and grow section. After you have completed all twelve months in the previous section, begin a new page in your journal by titling it "Learn and Grow." Think of all the things you did *not* accomplish that you intended to. This is not labeling them as failures, but it is anything you did not accomplish or that you did not complete. What can you learn from them? How can you grow? What will you do differently moving forward? How can this serve you in the future? Is it still important to you? What got in the way? How will you overcome the challenges in the future? For each item you list, ask yourself these questions and write the answers next to each item. By doing this exercise, it will prevent you from making the same mistakes repeatedly this new year.

3. **Step Three**—Complete your goal review checklist. Ideally, you would have last year's goals in a previous journal, and next to each goal, you would put a box. From there, you can literally check the box and give yourself a sense of accomplishment for each goal you set for yourself and accomplished. Lastly, when you complete this task in your previous year's journal, you transfer those accomplishments into your new journal and list the specific goals you *did* attain last year. This allows you to finish on a positive note, so you are reminded of the wins and successes from the previous year.

PART TWO—PLANNING FOR NEXT YEAR

1. **Step One**—"Goal storm." You have heard of brainstorming, but now you are going to do a goal-storming exercise. To do this properly, do not worry about whether you can complete them in this calendar year. If it is something you want to achieve in your life, then write it down. There are no limits and no judgment during this exercise. Position yourself somewhere with no distractions, maybe put on some inspirational music, go wherever you need to, and get in your zone. Fill up as much as you can on the goal storm activity. Do not let your pen leave the paper. Where do you want to travel? What car do you want to drive? What does your dream home look like? What dream job are you pursuing? What business do you want to start? What relationships do you want to have? Who are you closest to? What does your faith and spirituality look like? What is your health and physical fitness like? What charity organization are you serving? How many people are you helping? The list goes on, so let your mind wander. If done correctly, this may take you a long time, and you may have pages full of things listed.

2. **Step Two**—Categorize your goal storm notes. Some examples of categories could be spiritual, travel, health, family, relationships, finance, business, philanthropy, and entertainment. Scrub your list and place each goal into your categories. To give you a general range, you might have five to ten goals per category however there is no limit. The more you can come up with, the better!

3. **Step Three**—Create your top five to ten list. These are the ones you really want to accomplish this year. These are likely the goals that have the most impact, importance, and influence over all the rest of the goals. These are the ones you would achieve to consider it a home run year. This forces you to narrow the focus and go from the floodlight of having a hundred goals to putting the magnifying glass on them. This is going to be one of the most challenging parts because you may be tempted to want it all now. To avoid that temptation, go back to the focusing questions to establish your priorities and get S.M.A.R.T. with these goals.

This entire process will take time. It may easily take eight to ten hours to reflect on the previous year, creating your new goals, reviewing, narrowing down, and planning. You may be thinking, *seriously*? I am very serious. This is your life. There is nothing more important. Apply the same enthusiasm you have when cheering on your favorite sports team or planning that dream vacation. This will challenge you to think about who you must become, what training you need, and who you need to surround yourself with.

If you do both exercises, you are on the right track. It does not guarantee you will hit them, but it gives you a massive advantage compared to most people because you wrote them down and created a plan. Your goals are merely a wish until you write them down. Success comes down to three things: goals, strategies, and action. These exercises accomplish the first part. Now, it comes down to developing the strategies and taking massive action. The template for this exercise is in the Chapter 2 section of the Cannonball Workbook.

No Body Likes a Playground Bully

"Haters are my motivators."

ELLEN DEGENERES

Everything we have discussed so far can sound good, yet the final piece of the puzzle in preparation for goal setting and dreaming big is equipping yourself for battle. We must be willing to fight for what we believe in. We must build a bunker around ourselves that does not allow the enemy to penetrate our turf. I distinctly remember going public on social media with a goal of mine regarding the achievement of financial success. I was willing to put it out into the world for accountability and visibility. Immediately, the post was met with comments from people judging my goals, casting stones at my real motivations, and, in essence, wanting to see me fail. I realized that putting myself out there in a vulnerable and transparent way resulted in keyboard warriors coming out and revealing their insecurities on my post. By highlighting my aspirations and seeking the support of my friends, it ended up revealing that some of them were not my friends after all. Some of them would rather see me fail so they could say, "I told you so," instead of seeing me win and finding inspiration from my efforts.

What I realized is that if we cannot celebrate someone else's wins, then we are not mature enough yet to handle our own. My dreams needed to be protected and supported by other like-minded and positive people who wanted to see me win just as much as I wanted to see them win. The same is true for all of us. The minute we put ourselves out there in good faith, we will encounter opposition. At times, it may come from unlikely suspects within our family or close circle. We must remember that at the start of each day, we should put on our armor. We are going into battle and will be constantly tested. The forces of average will try and knock us off our game, and we must have the resolve and fortitude to keep going despite what others may think or say. We must proceed anyway because we said we would. We must keep going because, at the end of the day, it is not their dream but ours. I firmly believe God did not place these dreams in our hearts if He did not also equip us with the capacity to overcome the challenges.

Do not let the dream stealers or playground bullies try to prevent you from going after what you want. Do not stop and listen to every dog who barks at you along the way. This is your journey, and that is all that matters. My favorite book of all time is *The Traveler's Gift*[5] by Andy Andrews. In there, he says, "Those who are critical of my goals and dreams simply do not understand the higher purpose to which I have been called." Get clear on what you want, why you want it, and go pursue it unapologetically.

QUESTIONS TO CONSIDER:

1. What do I really want?
2. What about that is important to me?
3. Who do I need to surround myself with to support my dreams?
4. What relationship do I need to distance myself from?
5. What are my top three priorities to accomplish my dreams?

6. Who can I speak with who has accomplished what I desire?

7. What mindset do I need to have to achieve my dreams?

8. What skillsets do I need to acquire to achieve my dreams?

9. What daily habits do I need to adopt to achieve my dreams?

10. How can I protect my mindset so no playground bullies will deter me from achieving my dreams?

STOP AND COMPLETE:

Create your "live list" (often referred to as a bucket list). Space is provided in your Cannonball Workbook to fill this in. Years ago, one of my mentors opened my eyes to the concept of the live list. Rather than working hard all our lives, up until the point of retirement, and then checking off the experiences, places, and things we want to do before we die—he took a different approach. He encouraged us to develop a list of all the experiences, places, and things we wanted to do now to make life more meaningful and enjoyable. Why put everything we want to experience on hold? Why not live life to the fullest now?

In this exercise, I want you to have fun and imagine a world where there are no limits. Dare to dream boldly and not let money, time, or knowledge prevent you from writing down what you want. Imagine you have all the time, money, and knowledge in the world to make anything possible. What would you do? Where would you go? What would you have? What would you want to experience? List everything that comes to mind in the categories below, and remember, there are no limits so breakthrough those limiting beliefs or false justifications and let your child-like spirit come through. It is not about the money; it is about what the money can do. Money simply magnifies the person you are so let your true self shine.

CHAPTER 3

YOU CAN HAVE YOUR CAKE AND EAT IT TOO

"Nothing is impossible, the word itself says 'I'm possible.'"

AUDREY HEPBURN

THE POWER OF THE WORD "YET"

In the fall of 2020, I was getting home from a typical workday when my wife shared a story with me regarding our oldest daughter, who was in first grade at the time. She told me how she picked her up from school and, like always, asked her during the car ride home what the best part of her day was. However, the answer on this day was unlike any other previously. It was not about a game they played at recess or some funny joke a friend told in the lunchroom. This day, our daughter told my wife that the favorite part of her day was in class because they were learning about a "growth mindset." First, kudos to the teacher for teaching the kids an amazing topic like that! Of course, I emailed the teacher that night and told her how amazing I thought it was and how it aligned so well with what we teach at home and what I do for work daily. But if that answer was not enough, my wife told me how our oldest daughter elaborated even further. She proceeded to tell her that she learned how the word "yet" is a good word. The example provided by my daughter, who loves horse riding, was she can confidently say something like, "I know how to ride a horse." However, she followed that up, saying, "I do not know how to feed a horse yet."

Step back and think about this for a moment. How amazing is this? In first grade, our daughter was learning about a growth mindset, how the word "yet" is a good word, and tying that together with something she loves, like horses. She knows how to ride a horse, but she does not know how to feed a horse yet. If you wanted an example of how to melt my heart and blow my mind at the same time, then there it is. The wisdom in that short example is priceless, and thinking my daughter was learning this in school, let alone coming home to share it with us, was incredible. I learned just as much that day. Often, we set goals around what we want to achieve and the things we want to have, yet our own thinking can get in the way when we focus more on what we do not have versus appreciating what we do. The power of one word like "yet" can shift our entire perspective. Whatever you are pursuing right now and have not attained, remember this simple lesson. It is not that you haven't been successful; it is just that you have not obtained your ultimate outcome yet.

BEING IN THE RIGHT ROOM

In early 2016, I attended a company event in North Carolina that changed my life forever. During this event, I was in a room full of hundreds of high achievers, and everyone was learning about how to expand their real estate businesses across different states. This expansion model was innovative at the time because, traditionally, real estate agents were restricted to conducting business in their local markets. However, challenging the status quo and removing artificial barriers now created an opportunity others had not seen before. It demonstrated the power of thinking without limits. Because I have always been a sponge and extremely coachable, if I'm shown something once, I will usually understand it quickly and act upon it even quicker.

This event proved to be the birthplace of our business, The Locker Room. That day, I began to filter information and process how I could apply it to creating a coaching platform that could apply to real estate offices across North America. I was taking the same models and systems that real estate agents were learning from and figuring out how they could apply to a coaching business. I left that event with a sense of conviction I never had before. I began to ask myself the "what if" questions mentioned in Chapter 2. In fact, I created an exercise called a "question mind" that you will be asked to do at the end of this chapter. It forced me to think without limits. It allowed me to break through barriers that previously existed. The power of thinking beyond the traditional scope gave me a vision that has now led to impact tens of thousands of lives. Just when we feel like we are thinking big, we step back, ask questions, and realize we are just getting started. There is a much bigger vision awaiting us if we are willing to take the time to explore and think without limits.

LESSONS AND SUCCESS PRINCIPLES
Programming Our Internal Operating System

Stories like the ones I just shared shine the light on thinking without limits. Whether we add the word "yet" to the end of our sentences or expose ourselves to new information that opens our eyes to possibilities, we owe it to ourselves to expand our thinking, so we do not become the lid to our own success.

Where do we begin? How do we ensure we are not putting ourselves in a box? How do we operate under the limitless thinking success principle? The answer begins with a proven model. To illustrate the model, first, consider something you probably use daily such as your computer or smartphone. When you purchase a new computer, it comes preloaded with software, applications, templates, and a standard operating system. Furthermore, the computer is made up of hardware components such as the RAM, which dictates the capacity for memory on the computer. It also comes with hardware components such as a processor, which provides instructions and processing power that the computer needs to do its work. Once we begin using the computer, we may begin to install other applications that will impact the amount of memory and capacity of the processor to do its job. Occasionally, we may install a file that contains a virus, and suddenly, the computer is not able to function the way it had when it was brand new.

This analogy demonstrates the point. When we are born, we are much like a brand-new computer. We have an internal operating system and capacity for memory storage. The older we get, the more we begin to download new information, and occasionally, that information contains a virus. That virus can inhibit the functionality of our internal systems, and we may never go back and install the proper software, in other words, the proper thought processes to get rid of that virus. Therefore, the virus sits in our internal operating system and creates bugs, preventing us from operating at full capacity.

The good news is that it is not too late. It is possible to examine our operating system and get rid of the viruses. We can reprogram ourselves to adopt a new operating system that is more efficient and has the capacity for more storage. We control the ability to delete old files and replace them with new files. To do this, we must first understand how those files got there in the first place. Fill in the blank for me on these statements. Money does not grow on _____. The love of money is the root of all _____. Success lives outside of your comfort _____. If you successfully answered trees, evil, and zone, then, congratulations, you are like 99.9% of the population who can relate to what it means to have a default set of programming. And yet, when was the last time you ever challenged those thoughts? When was the last time you ever questioned where you got those beliefs from in the first place?

In my experience, it began early in life from well-intended parents or teachers who said these things to protect us. However, those statements were instantly adopted as truths by many and shaped their programming, which influenced their entire operating system. No wonder many people dance around the topic of money. We have been taught from a young age that it does not come in abundance, and it is the root of bad things. Many of the beliefs fueling our operating systems were given to us by people projecting their own limiting beliefs on us. We were too young at the time to question or challenge the thought because our minds were too immature, so we ended up adopting those beliefs as our own truths. This has become the single greatest game of telephone known to mankind.

Furthermore, when we were introduced to these beliefs without challenging them, our conscious and sub-conscious minds began to find evidence supporting them. We created these files in our minds associated with a particular experience in our lives and then assigned a belief or attached an emotion to it. For example, if we are in sales, we may associate lead generation with the feeling of being slimy, salesy, and inconveniencing our friends. Who wants to hear from us? Have we stopped to wonder where this came from in the first place? Is it true? We may realize that twenty years ago we were having a bad day, and during that bad day, the phone rang. We picked up the phone, only to be greeted by a telemarketer who was trying to sell us something and would not accept no for an answer. Frustrated and annoyed, we hung up the phone and immediately let out a frustrated scream. Ever since then, we have received countless phone calls from other telemarketers attempting to sell us the latest and greatest product and every time we hung up on them. This created a pattern. Our beliefs about things can be influenced by the frequency of the action and intensity of the emotion surrounding them. In this case, a bad day from twenty years ago has now resulted in us believing that making calls for lead generation is bad. We may believe that we are annoying everyone, no one wants to hear from us, and we will probably get hung up on anyway.

Can you relate? This common example sets us up because all of that is true or none of that is true, depending on what *you* choose to believe. Is it true that calling and trying to help people is bad? Is it true that everyone is going to respond the same way you did twenty years ago? Is it true you are inconveniencing people? Is it true they do not want to hear from you? When you think about it and ask the questions, it can sound sort of silly, right?

The model I personally use, along with many other industry leaders, is under the acronym of P.T.F.A.R.

P = Programming
T = Thoughts
F = Feelings
A = Actions
R = Results

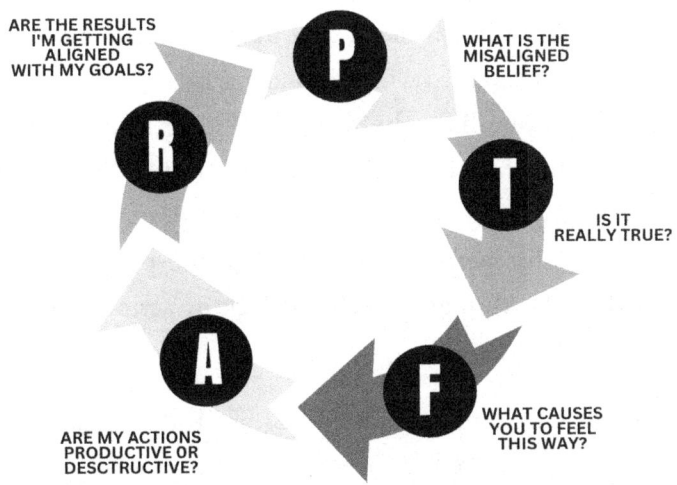

PTFAR
PROGRAMMING - THOUGHTS - FEELINGS - ACTIONS - RESULTS

Put simply, our programming leads to our thoughts. Our thoughts lead to our feelings. Our feelings lead to our actions. Our actions lead to our results. The best part of this model is that it provides a formula for us to self-evaluate and re-write our programming in a methodical way. The success hack I have learned using this model is to reverse engineer the sequence. For the sake of example, let us assume we are not achieving a desired outcome such as selling three homes per month in real estate. We go to our coach who recognizes we are completely focused on the "R" in this model. They ask questions about our activities. They ask us what we are or are not doing that is causing us not to achieve our desired result? In this case, we respond with, we are not proactively lead generating because we do not want to bother our friends. If we continue to reverse the order of the model, the next question would be to ask us what our feelings are when it comes to lead generation. We respond saying we feel like we are bothering people, and we feel they would be annoyed if we reached out to them. The next coaching question would be around our thoughts. We may be asked to share what we think of when hearing the words lead generation. Likely, we instantly respond by saying we think it is slimy, salesy, and disingenuous. We think it is self-serving and it is about trying to make a sale. We proceed to tell our coach that no one likes the feeling of being sold to, so, in our mind, the thought of picking up the phone and calling someone is not an attractive option. Lastly, our coach repeats all the answers we gave and asks for permission to explore the programming that may have led to the thoughts, feelings, lack of action, and the lack of results.

Programming is where the real work begins. The challenge is taking years of beliefs, supported by frequency and emotion, and then, trying to unravel it all to reprogram our belief system. Just like a gardener trying to get rid of all the weeds in their garden, it cannot be achieved by picking the weeds at the surface level. It takes digging and reaching all the way down to pull them out at the root. Those roots can run very deep and very wide so that when we tug on them, initially, it seems like there is no give. The gardener may be tempted to trim off what can be seen or spray to kill the weeds. These actions are not addressing the root of the issue that lies beneath the surface.

Our minds have had this programming embedded for years; therefore, some quick fix remedy or surface level adjustment won't cut it. We must spend time evaluating deep places that we may have never explored before. This is where the true magic lies. When we can get to the root of the issue, we are liberated to rewrite the programming. When we do this, everything after it changes because we have written new code for our internal operating system. Wayne Dyer said, "If you change the way you look at things, the things you look at change." He is speaking directly to the programming of our minds. And it is in our control to develop the proper programming, so our operating systems function the way we need them to. At the programming level, it changes the way we think about something, which changes our feelings towards it. If our feelings change, then, our actions change, which ultimately yield us a different result.

Lastly, once we do this, we are now deploying our Reticular Activating System or R.A.S. We may identify this with the last time we purchased that dream car and drove it off the lot. We could not believe it because the dealer even had available the color we always wanted. Head held high, we drove off to showcase the new vehicle, and we instantly encountered another one just like it on the road. Thinking it must have been a coincidence, we kept driving toward home, so we could show off the new car to our family. Next thing we knew, we passed another and then another. Same year, same model, and even the same color. It must be a conspiracy, right? Wrong. The likelihood is those vehicles were always there. They probably always drove on that same stretch of road, during the same time of day, heading to or from work. The only difference now is our R.A.S. has been deployed. We are now seeing something we had never seen before, but yet it was there all along.

This is how powerful our brains can be. They are machines that can work to our favor or our detriment. When we choose to focus on something and apply the right frequency and emotion behind it, we able to manipulate the programming. When we change our programming, now, our brain is activated to find the supporting evidence to back us up. This can be wonderful when reprogramming our minds because, when we have worked through all the viruses and eliminated them, our minds will get to work again to support the new belief system. We will see things we never saw before, and it will build our confidence to take bold action. It will change the way we think and feel about something because, now, it is supported with positive programming. Ultimately, it will yield us the results we desire. After all, the definition of insanity is doing the same thing over and over and expecting different results. Apply the P.T.F.A.R. method and get to the root of the issue, so everything thereafter becomes a conscious choice rather than an unconscious belief system that may have been adopted without your conscious consent.

Become the Person Who Has What You Desire

To build the skill of limitless thinking, I refer to a previous leader that I was in business with. She would always share the mantra of how we must first become the person we need to be, and then do the things that person needs to do to have what that person has. If my goal is to make a million dollars per year, I need to first become the person who makes a million dollars in a year. What would that look like? How does that person act daily? What is their mindset like? How do they deal with big responsibilities? How do they view the world? What books do they read? As I work on becoming that person, I then shift my focus to doing what that person does. What does a person who makes a million dollars per year do? What are their daily habits?

What do they prioritize? How do they manage rejection? How do they go about networking and making connections? What activities represent the top twenty percent? What does their daily calendar look like? Finally, the achievement phase comes into play. Once I have become the person and do what it takes daily, I can expect to achieve the results they achieve.

The challenge for most of us is our unwillingness to commit to the process. We want to have all the results without necessarily doing the work, let alone becoming the person playing at that level of success. Often, we seek the shortcut or get rich quick approach. We live in a society that prizes instant gratification, to the point where a goldfish has a longer attention span than a human. If we talk to enough high achievers, we will hear their success was a process over an extended period, not overnight.

It is no different than an Olympic athlete. Imagine turning on the television every four years to witness the best athletes in the world competing. We get to sit in our comfortable chairs while they perform on the world stage. We see them compete for just a few seconds and think to ourselves, *wow, they are lucky; they make it look so easy; or it just seems to come naturally to them.* What we do not get to see is all the blood, sweat, and tears they have shed during the four years leading up to the games. We do not witness them getting up before dawn to go train, swimming in the pool sixteen hours per day, or studying game films. We do not sit at the dinner table with them and see what their nutrition plan is like. All we see are the results, which, for the elite, is an Olympic medal around their neck.

The secret to being a world-class leader and having that type of success is in the work that no one sees. They first had to *become* Olympic athletes. They had to work on their mindset and prepare themselves for the endurance and challenges that lay ahead. They had to commit themselves to a superhuman regime that most cannot fathom just to get their bodies in peak physical condition. Only then could they have an invitation to perform at a world champion level. We must recognize this and evaluate the validity of our expectations. We should not expect to have the things we desire without first becoming the person who deserves that success. We should not expect to have the things we desire without understanding the work required of us and what others who achieve that level of success do every single day. When we can stare reality in the face and accept what is expected of us, then, limitless thinking and commitment to the process can co-exist.

To take things a step further, everything rises and falls on our mindset. The common denominator for success is how everything starts with a mindset. Without a proper mindset, our thinking will be limited, and our results will fall short of our true potential. I remember, back in 2007, when I was first introduced to audiobooks. My friend handed me one by Donny Deutsch called, *The Big Idea*. Little did I know at the time, I would become addicted to personal growth and development from then on. My car became a library on wheels because I turned off the radio and began to feed my mind with empowering information. I did not realize what I was doing until years later, but I was working on myself. I had to become the person first, then do the things necessary to achieve what I wanted to achieve. In this book, I distinctly remember a part when he said, "… there has to be a better way." He kept repeating that line, and I sunk my teeth in. It kept me awake at night, knowing I was restless and there was more to life than what I was currently doing. Indeed, there had to be a better way.

That single phrase from the book ignited my entire entrepreneurial journey. I bought a business planning book and began to go to the library on my off days to read and fill out a business plan. I had an awakening that my idea of entrepreneurship was becoming a reality because I was ready. My mindset was ready. If I tried starting a business previously, I would not have been equipped to handle the responsibilities that go along with it. It gave me the confidence to step out in faith and launch "The Player's Edge," an indoor baseball training facility that I opened in my home state of Illinois. I was living in Florida at the time, working for a large Fortune 500 company, and was tired of working for someone else. I was tired of going to Monday morning sales meetings, where our sales manager would constantly say, "The man without a plan will always work for the man with a plan." I wanted out. I knew there was more. Plus, entrepreneurship ran in my family. I leveraged The Player's Edge as a reason to move back home to be closer to family and begin my first venture. All of this started by listening to a personal growth audiobook that a friend handed to me. I have never looked back and have consumed thousands of hours of audiobooks ever since.

How can we take these concepts and put them into action? My encouragement is to develop a personal growth plan. A personal growth plan is arguably more important than a business plan. Traditional thinking would have us believe we must focus on the tactical elements of running a business. We need to become a spreadsheet jockey. Even in the space of leadership and coaching, most focus on helping others achieve the results they themselves want to achieve. They help people set goals and action items to achieve those goals. All of that is warranted and I spend a lot of time doing that with others too. Yet do not miss the critical point I am making. While most of us set goals of what we want to achieve and action plans to achieve those goals, when is the last time we set a goal on who we need to *become*? We may have the business plan and financial forecasts down to a science, but where is the pro forma on us as a leader? What can others expect of us as we continue to grow? How will we develop as a leader a year from today?

The best way to do this is to take a monthly calendar and have a blank area with one square for each month. When you have all twelve months ready, fill them with all the personal growth and development plans you have. Beginning with the end in mind, what area of your life do you want to improve on over the next year? When you have that answer, it is time to reverse engineer who you need to become and what you need to do to become that individual.

Here are some questions to consider when completing each month:

1. What book do I need to read or listen to that aligns with my personal growth goal?

2. What conference, seminar, or training must I attend?

3. Who do I need to hire as a mentor or coach?

4. What blogs, articles, or magazines must I subscribe to and read?

5. What accountability do I need to insert to complete each item?

6. What networking events do I need to attend?

7. What scorecard do I need to create to measure my success?

8. Who is the personal board of directors in my life that I will accept accountability from?

If you answer these questions and execute your monthly personal growth plan, I can assure you that the person you are a year from now will look entirely different from the person you are today. To quote Thomas Jefferson, "If you want something you've never had, you must be willing to do something you've never done." By committing to personal growth, you are directly influencing your level of thinking. The same level of thinking that got you to where you are today is not the same level of thinking it will take to get you where you intend to go. A template has been provided in your Cannonball Workbook to complete a twelve-month personal growth plan calendar.

Remember, this is a journey. Be kind to yourself. Commit to personal growth and become the person you must become to achieve the things you desire to achieve. If your version of success has not been achieved yet, then resort back to the magic word of my oldest daughter—yet. Keep going, keep working on yourself, and take bold actions that align with your goals. Your programming is in your control. Get rid of the viruses in your operating system, and when you do that, everything else will change.

QUESTIONS TO CONSIDER:

1. Who do I need to become to achieve what I desire?

2. What do high achievers do who have already accomplished what I seek?

3. How can I apply the P.T.F.A.R. model in my life right now?

4. What positive habits are currently serving my limitless thinking?

5. What self-sabotaging habits are currently holding me back?

6. What area of my life can I reframe by using the word "yet"?

7. Who can hold me accountable for my personal growth plan?

8. What area of my programming can I identify now that needs work?

9. How can I best position myself for success when I create a new set of programming?

10. Where has the reticular activating system shown up in my life?

STOP AND COMPLETE:

We have spoken a lot about limitless thinking, thinking about possibilities instead of obstacles, and reprogramming our belief systems so they work for us rather than against us. I want you to do a "Question Mind" exercise with me now, utilizing questions that begin with "What if…?".

In this section, the rules of engagement are you must think and write in the form of questions. Those questions must begin with the words "What if." In the Cannonball Workbook, there are twenty spaces, so do not stop until you have at least twenty questions written. Expand your thinking, allow your mind to wander, and give yourself permission to think limitlessly.

CHAPTER 4

SUCCESS LIVES OUTSIDE YOUR COMFORT ZONE IS B.S.

"One can have no smaller or greater mastery than mastery of oneself."

LEONARDO DA VINCI

THE $1,100 IDEA

During the summer of 2023, our company hosted a national event in Orlando, Florida. My wife and I decided to bring our two daughters with us to experience the event, followed by a brief vacation since we were already going to be there. Leading up to the event, our daughters had been through training at the local Humane Society to help with the animals. As you may remember, many of their answers when asked what they wanted to be when they grew up revolved around animals. They have a huge heart for animals and want to serve them however they can. The girls said they wanted a booth in the back of the event space like the other sponsors did. They proceeded to tell my wife and me that they wanted to make bracelets and sell them for one dollar, and all the money would be donated to the local Humane Society. Naturally, we said yes and purchased the supplies, including a tablecloth, signage placeholders, and all the necessities for this philanthropic venture.

They were so excited, and, in my mind, I was simply proud of them for being entrepreneurial. Generally, they are shy in front of people, so I knew this would make them open up around our friends too. I did not know what to expect, but it was just something neat for them to do and we supported it enthusiastically. When the event began, our daughters were rushing to make sure the table was set up perfectly and ready for bracelet orders. I made an announcement from the stage, and what happened next surpassed my wildest expectations. The audience stormed the table throughout the event, and they were taking orders for a one-dollar bracelet from nearly everyone in attendance. We even had people walking up handing them twenty and one-hundred-dollar bills to support the donation to our local Humane Society. By the end of the event, the girls had raised over $1,100 and could not wait to get home to present the money to the local Humane Society.

As a proud father, I was humbled and profoundly impacted by what they had just accomplished. I was so grateful for the support our attendees showed the girls during those few days. I was also stunned at what those two had just pulled off. I could not help but think how a few days earlier, they had an idea, executed it, and now raised over $1,100 to support something they're wildly passionate about. Not one second was spent worrying about what others might think. They never concerned themselves with how much money they would raise. It could have been ten dollars, and they would have been happy. It shook me to my core and helped me realize the girls were so passionate and enthusiastic about helping the animals that everything else took care of itself. They were operating in their strength zone and were never uncomfortable. They were too busy doing something they loved and having fun to worry about anything else. They aligned their passion with a purpose, and people from all over North America rallied behind them to support the cause. That is what operating within our strength zone can look like.

YOU NEVER KNOW WHO IS WATCHING

In the summer of 2000, between my junior and senior years of high school, I was preparing to play an American Legion Baseball game in Farmington, Illinois. A lot of scouting efforts were ramping up from colleges in the area as I was approaching my final year of high school. This game was at night, and I was set to be the starting pitcher. I was always a multi-position player, so, when I was not pitching, I was playing first base. Prior to the game starting, I was down in the bullpen, warming up for the game. I noticed two college scouts were in attendance and positioned themselves behind home plate to see me pitch. One was from a D1 university in the area, and another from a competitive junior college. Yet just as I was finishing my warmups, I noticed a man get out of his car and walk toward the baseball field in a straw hat, khaki pants, and a polo shirt. He also carried a black leather bag, which made me assume he was also a scout. I had never seen him before, but if you have been around scouts long enough, you can spot them out of the crowd. I did not think anything of it and joined my team to huddle up before taking the field.

I ended up having one of the best games of my entire summer. I pitched a complete game one-hitter and went three for four batting with two home runs. When the game was finished, the man I noticed prior to the game walked up to me and stuck out his hand to shake mine. While we shook hands, he proceeded to introduce himself and mentioned that he was a scout for the Major League Scouting Bureau. If you are not familiar with them, they have a select number of scouts who operate within separate regions of the United States on behalf of all thirty Major League Baseball teams. That game changed my life forever. The gentleman ended up scheduling a time to visit my home so I could run through a series of eye tests and assessments. My senior year never had a single game without at least eight Major League scouts in attendance. I got drafted by the Oakland A's™ in the eighteenth round of the Major League Baseball 2001 Draft.

Pause for a moment; that one game changed my entire life. I had the right game in front of the right person at the right time. Scouts do not go into a game looking for reasons to like you. There is plenty of talent out there for them to see, and they are looking for reasons to cross you off their list. Assume for a moment I had the same game, but what would have happened if I kicked the dirt or yelled a curse word when the player got a hit off me? What would have happened if the one at bat I did not get a hit on, I ended up slamming my helmet on the ground or showing up my teammates? I could have had the exact same game, but if I behaved in a manner inconsistent with what scouts look for, he would have crossed me off the list and gotten back into his car to head up the road. We never know who is watching. Right now, we may be struggling or tempted to express our frustrations. We never know who is watching our game, and it only takes one time to have the game of our life in front of the right person to change our future forever.

The story does not end there. I later learned that this man had no intention of coming to see me. Earlier that day, he flew into Chicago to see a player in the area on his scouting list. He had rented a car to drive down to see another player in the St. Louis area the next day. It was during his drive about halfway through that he saw lights on at a baseball field in the middle of Illinois. He was ready to stretch his legs, so he decided to pull his car over and see the game. It was my game. You cannot make this up. It was an "accident" that he stumbled upon me, but I was able to have one of the best games of my entire summer that night in front of the right person. You never know who is watching.

Lastly, I did not try to be someone I wasn't. I did not try to fake it until I made it. I did my business knowing people were there to scout me and played my heart out like any other game. In other words, I chose to operate in my strength zone rather than trying to find success outside of my comfort zone. One of the best parts of the whole story is how my MLB 2001 Draft report said the following, "Free, easy swing. Hits with strong, quick hands and wrists. Good bat. Likes to play." The last part that mentions "likes to play" is the first I have ever seen on a draft report for a player. What this tells me is that I played with heart and emotion and left it all out on the field that even scouts noticed how much fun I was having by just being myself and playing to my strengths.

LESSONS AND SUCCESS PRINCIPLES
Expand Your Strength Zone

One of the greatest success principles I have observed through my children as well as myself is that success starts by identifying our strengths and working to expand them. We have likely heard the adage, "Success lives outside our comfort zone." I subscribed to this belief system for a long time because smart and successful people said it, so it had to be true. I began to interrogate the reality of this when I was going through a challenging time in a leadership role. As the CEO of a large real estate office, I worked tirelessly to recruit agents, manage staff, control finances, and the never-ending list of responsibilities that came with the territory. I had a breaking point when the recruiting aspect was never enough. When one month would end, the new month would begin, and it was a vicious cycle of top-down pressure to perform. It never seemed like I could win because of the constant stress of bringing in a certain number of new real estate agents monthly.

I was doing all the right things but felt out of alignment with my style and values. I had subscribed to the belief that success lives outside my comfort zone, so I always wrote it off as doing the right thing since I was constantly uncomfortable. However, where is the line drawn? I was burned out, unsatisfied with my daily work, and doing things that made me uncomfortable. I would dread going to work every day and finally decided to challenge my own thinking. I went through the P.T.F.A.R. model for myself and realized my programming was the problem. I had subscribed to this belief because it had been repeated by many others I respected. Was it really true, though? Did success really have to live outside of my comfort zone? Was that really what I would accept for the rest of my life?

To find the answer I sought to reprogram my belief system, I had to ask some additional questions first. One of those questions was, "What is *my* definition of success?" This is one of the most common questions people rarely have a clear answer to. Unfortunately for many, they are pursuing success yet have no idea how to even define it for themselves. One thing is for certain, though, they are pretty sure they do not have it. If I asked fifty people to answer that question, I would get fifty different answers. Some may be similar, but the odds of fifty different and unique responses are highly probable. For most, it involves money. They define success by the amount of money in their bank account. When they speak about successful people, they are really saying how that person earns a lot of money. Listen, if your definition of success is how much money you have, then nothing is wrong with that. I am certainly not here to judge. I tend to believe there Is more to It than just money. What If we had all the money we dreamed of, but our relationships were empty? What if we had all the money we dreamed of, but our health was suffering? Is our definition of success truly just about the money?

Your first responsibility Is to define *your* definition of success. Once you can do this, circle back to the original question. Does *your* definition of success have to live outside of your comfort zone? What success means to you is different than your neighbor, so why are you continuously comparing yourself to them? Why do you feel their success creates a lack of success available to you? When I took this journey, I realized that my version of success differed from everyone else, which was okay! I did not need to explain it, justify it, or defend it. It was completely mine. From there, the reprogramming could begin because I stopped operating with a herd mentality. I could finally answer my question.

If success does not have to live outside of my comfort zone, then where does it live? Another way of asking this question is, how can I capitalize on my strengths to achieve my definition of success? How can I recognize what I am great at and equally recognize what I am not so great at? What are the activities that I enjoy that give me energy compared to the activities I do not enjoy and deplete my energy? Asking these questions gave me a sense of hope and liberation that

I was not crazy. I had been through a phase of life where I tried to fake it until I made it. I pursued a success defined by the amount of money I was earning. It all felt empty, but the minute I established my new belief system, I became empowered and unapologetic. I was clear on what success meant and how I would achieve it. Success does not have to live outside of our comfort zone. I would submit that the definition of success lies in expanding our strength zone. What is the strength zone? I have broken it into three phases, as seen in the illustration.

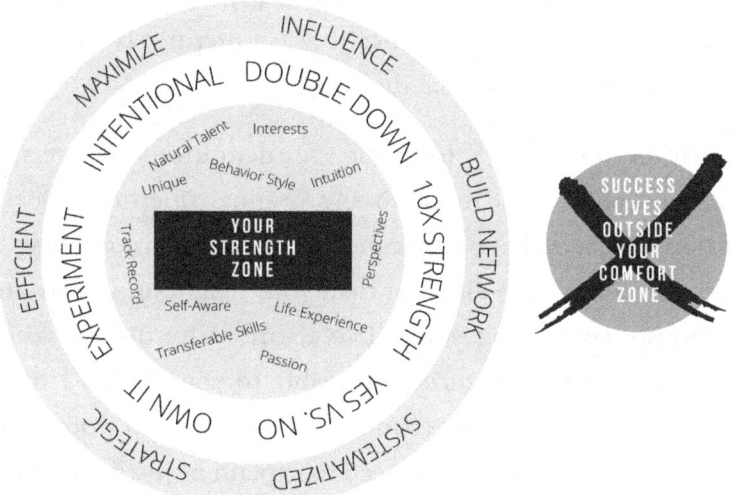

Begin by looking at the center ring. This is the bullseye or core of what makes you unique. The first step is to identify your strengths and own them completely. It requires you to be honest with yourself and dig deep internally. God gave you a distinct set of talents and gifts unlike anyone else. The inner circle represents those unique abilities that are waiting for you to recognize them and tap into them completely. The center ring consists of things like your natural behavior style. You may have taken an assessment like the D.I.S.C assessment, which gives insight into your natural behavioral style and how you can apply that to your daily life, and rather than apologizing for how you are, you lean even further into your greatness. The inner circle also includes things like your transferrable skills from prior careers. Stop discounting your previous career experiences and begin recognizing what you were good at. How can you take those skills and apply them to what you are doing today?

If you spend too much time on social media, you will see images circulating that demonstrate how success lives outside your comfort zone and only the top two percent of people are operating consistently with that of someone who is successful. It argues that most people are just living a life of complacency, accepting mediocrity, unmotivated, and are unable to attain success almost as if there is a finite amount available. Do not let this become your programming. Your version of success lies within you by capitalizing on your strength zone. Everything in the inner circle combines to create an amazing recipe that is you. It is your unique talents, strengths, and passions that need to be recognized. Do not worry about what you consider a weakness; focus on what you consider a strength. You are now ready to expand your strength zone.

The second ring from the center is the beginning of expansion. Without recognizing and owning our strengths, we can never begin to expand our strength zone. This second ring is where magic begins because we can utilize our unique gifts in ways we never have before. This leads to a higher degree of clarity and confidence. When we apply those to our recipe, we can double down our efforts since we are not concerned about being good at everything, and we accept that we only need to be great at a few things. We will operate with a heightened sense of awareness and intentionality than ever before. This allows us to experiment more by utilizing our strengths, which leads to new breakthroughs and ideas that would have never been possible before while operating within a box. Our decision-making becomes clearer because we recognize what to say yes and no to. The old days of saying yes to everything are gone because we are now working towards self-mastery. If someone else can do a better job because it fits into their strength zone, then we can confidently say no and get back to our strength zone.

The final ring is where our strength zone really begins to expand. We become highly influential and surround ourselves with other influential people who balance out our weaknesses. We can build a network of high-minded individuals who each own their strengths and are completely content admitting their weaknesses. No one tries to fake it until they make it because we are all operating in alignment with our authentic selves. This allows us to be more systematized than ever before while entering a new level of strategic thinking. We are efficient and maximized to our fullest potential, which all stems from identifying and accepting what our success DNA truly looks like. We had the courage to say no to success being defined by constantly living outside our comfort zone because we were able to get clear on what success means to us, and we identified the strengths we can capitalize on to achieve that version of success.

The day I had this epiphany is the same day I took out a scratch piece of paper and created the diagram pictured here. It was a breakthrough moment for me, and maybe it is for you too. Ever since I realized this, I have felt liberated and broke off the chains that were holding me back. I no longer felt the need to be good at everything. I no longer had the pressures of dreading every day going into work. I no longer felt out of alignment doing things that felt uncomfortable. I found *my* way to achieve *my* version of success by using *my* strengths. The best version of yourself is waiting for you too, if you are willing to lean in.

Study the Game Film

"Amateurs practice until they get it right. Professionals practice until they cannot get it wrong."

UNKNOWN

Imagine for a moment, it is the final NFL game of the season. The energy is contagious, and billions of dollars are flowing on ads and marketing strategies. The players are practicing, having media days, and preparing for the big game. The two teams, who are about to go head-to-head, have worked all season to get to this point, and only one can be named the champion. Aside from practice, what do these championship-caliber teams also do throughout the week? They spend as much time in the war room studying game film as they do practicing. They are studying film on themselves and their teammates identifying missed opportunities, broken plays, missed blocks and tackles, and how they can be sharper when running the play again. They are also studying their opponent. They are looking for patterns, opportunities, and where they can expose their weaknesses to best capitalize. Practice and talent alone do not make a championship-caliber team. It is their ability to take the necessary time to analyze and study the game film that makes them elite. They are willing to slow things down on the front end to speed things up on the back end.

When watching a football game, what happens when a quarterback runs off the field after a turnover on downs? When the camera catches a glimpse of them sitting on the bench, generally, they have a tablet in their hand because they are watching the game film. They can identify what went right, what went wrong, and what they can do differently on the next play. Examples are all around us if we are just willing to take note of what the elite are doing. When was the last time we studied our own game film? When was the last time we were willing to replay the tape to identify what we are good at versus the areas where we may have opportunities for growth? An easy exercise to get in the habit of doing is K.I.S.S. In this case, it does not represent "keep it simple, stupid." The K.I.S.S. method can be applied to our daily, weekly, monthly, or quarterly routine to force us to study the game film.

K – WHAT DO I NEED TO **KEEP** DOING?

This makes us aware of what is producing the desired outcome we wish to have. Often, we may let the temptation to be creative deter us away from what is currently working. Success can be boring and repetitious, so we can double our efforts to answer this question.

I – WHAT DO I NEED TO BE MORE **INTENTIONAL** ABOUT?

This allows us to identify a skill set that will help us improve. It may also uncover other areas that need more intentionality, such as priority management, relationships, and activities.

S – WHAT DO I NEED TO **STOP** DOING?

Many times, we confuse activity and achievement. Knowing the difference between what is working and what is not can make all the difference in the world. Busyness can be the enemy of productivity, so use this as an opportunity to trim the busy work that does not align with the desired outcome.

S – WHAT DO I NEED TO **START** DOING?

What are we currently avoiding and making excuses for that we should just do? It's common to claim we don't know what to do when we know exactly what to do, but we overcomplicate things and then make excuses. Keep it simple.

Slowing down and answering these questions helps us study the game film to make in-game adjustments that align with our strengths. It is uncomfortable to keep going through the same motions over and over and expecting a different result. Take the time to be an elite champion at your craft and make the adjustments needed to achieve your goals. I have included a template in the Cannonball Workbook so you can apply these K.I.S.S. questions to various aspects of your life.

The 80/20 Principle

Knowing that success does not have to live outside of our comfort zone is the first step. Identifying our strength zone and working to expand it outwardly is the next step in the process. Being able to study our game film and make real-time adjustments that align with our strength zone only sharpens the saw so we can be more efficient. What is left is identifying what the core activities are that play to our strengths. This varies for everyone, but what is important is for us to understand the 80/20 principle and how it can apply.

If we went into our closet right now, would we say we probably only wear about twenty percent of the clothes in it? If we looked in our pantry, do we consume twenty percent of the food and the rest sits there and expires? If we took your industry and studied production, do twenty percent of the companies represent eighty percent of the results?

The 80/20 principle suggests that twenty percent of our activities are responsible for eighty percent of our results. Another way of saying this is that eighty percent of our activities are responsible for twenty percent of our results. The point is that not all things are weighted equally, and we must identify what top activities are responsible for most of the success we desire to achieve. Remember that twenty percent of activities need to be within our strength zone. If you were to share your calendar with me right now, what percentage of your time every week is spent working on your top-producing activities? Out of that percentage, what percentage of that time is in your strength zone?

Unfortunately, the number is extremely low for many. It is challenging for people to identify what their top twenty percent activities are in the first place, let alone make sure they are in their strength zone and consistently on their calendars. If you show me your calendar, I will be able to predict the level of achievement you have. Does your calendar reflect your goals and priorities? I cannot say I want to earn $100,000 in a year if my calendar represents the activities of someone who earns $30,000 per year.

A breakthrough moment for me was creating a formula that allowed me to analyze what my time was valued at. I had a new set of beliefs and programming that allowed me to operate in my strength zone without worrying about the rest, but something was missing. I needed to see the numbers and tap into the logical aspect of my brain. Emotionally, I was rejuvenated and connected to my daily activities supported by my unique strengths. However, now I needed to connect it from my heart to my head.

I created a worksheet called, "How Much is Your Time Worth?" and it was a huge awakening that reinforced my commitment to operating in my strength zone, prioritizing my top twenty percent activities, and pursuing my definition of success. It is included in your Cannonball Workbook. My hope is that you complete the exercise as well and experience a similar breakthrough as I did.

QUESTIONS TO CONSIDER:

1. How can implementing the K.I.S.S. questions benefit me?

2. What frequency am I going to study my own game film?

3. What specific area of my life or business do I need to study the game film right now?

4. Where has the 80/20 principle shown up in my life?

5. When was a time that I slowed down to reflect, and how did it help me move forward?

6. What are my thoughts on strength zone vs. comfort zone?

7. What are my strengths?

8. What activities give me energy?

9. What needs to change on my schedule to make room for my top twenty percent activities?

10. What realization stood out most from the "What is my time worth?" exercise?

STOP AND COMPLETE:

In 2022, I was inspired to create a keynote presentation for an event I was asked to speak at. I have since taught this course all over North America, and it is called "Turning Your Defining Moments into Your Superpowers." This worksheet is a byproduct of that keynote presentation, and I will ask you to complete it in the Cannonball Workbook. Life does not happen to us; it happens for us. This worksheet can serve as a catalyst for identifying your strength zone and leveraging it to achieve your definition of success.

CHAPTER 5

DO NOT BE THE SQUIRREL!

"We are what we repeatedly do. Excellence,
then, is not an act, but a habit."

ARISTOTLE

IT IS BECAUSE I HAD SPECIALIZED
SOCCER TRAINING

One day, our oldest daughter was talking to me about soccer. She was nine years old and had been asked to play on the 12U soccer team. She had only begun playing goalie the previous year and excelled quickly. Of course, as her father, I may be biased, but even many other parents went out of their way to tell us how well she was doing especially against girls three years older than her.

During our conversation, I asked her what sport she loves the most. Out of all the sports, she answered soccer, and so out of curiosity, I asked her why. She said, "It is because I have had specialized soccer training." Over the previous year, she had received one-on-one coaching lessons from an instructor for goalie training. What this did for her was unbelievable. Not only did her skillset improve, but most importantly, her confidence had as well. The combination of skillset plus confidence resulted in commitment. She was heavily committed to being the best goalie she could be for her team. There were games where my jaw dropped because of the athleticism and commitment she had to do what it took to win.

During the summer of 2023, the team finished first place in a large tournament in the Madison, Wisconsin area. They won the first game 13-0, the second game 3-1, and the third game 5-0 and secured the championship. They played against very good teams in the area, and one was notorious for being the soccer club where kids go if they want to play at the next level. An entire section of their website is dedicated to players who have gone on to play in college. Over the course of those games, our oldest daughter only allowed one goal. Yes, her team is incredible for supporting her, but out of all the shots and opportunities taken, only one goal slipped past her.

Commitment will be tested. One day after school, my daughter did not feel like going to goalie practice because she was tired. After thirty minutes of thinking, she decided to go without us forcing her because it did not feel right. Her exact words were, "I am good now. I was just overthinking it." This example illustrates what true commitment looks like. I watch her and am beyond proud. It has helped me realize the importance of having a commitment to *all* things. If we are going to do anything, we must do it the best that can be done. Raise the bar beyond our best, do it the best it can be done.

We can't just go through the motions, especially when others depend on us. It is a constant reminder during soccer weekends that I have much to learn from my daughter, especially when a skillset combined with confidence equals commitment.

IT IS TIME TO COME IN FOR DINNER

During junior high and high school, it was common in my neighborhood to hear my mom yell out the window that it was time to come in for dinner. The reason she had to constantly remind me was that I would lose all track of time while in the backyard hitting a baseball. It was not just any baseball. It was a makeshift setup where my dad tied a twenty-yard clothesline from one tree to another, and hanging from that clothesline by a metal clip was a baseball on a rope. I would slightly sway the rope so the ball would move as if a pitch was coming toward me. As soon as the pitch approached, I would take my best swing and see if I could hit it down to the other side of the clothesline. I knew if it went all the way to the other end, it was a perfect line drive hit right up the middle. If I pulled or mishit the ball, I would risk having my head crushed by the ball because the rope would go round and round to let me know my timing was off. After I hit the ball, I would walk down to the other end and do it all over again. I did this for hours every single day. I did not stay inside on a gaming system; I was out there putting in the work and making myself better for a sport that I loved.

I was committed to being the best player I could be. I constantly reminded myself of the doubters and skeptics and used that as fuel to get out and practice. Growing up, I attended the Illinois State University Baseball Winter Camps in Bloomington, Illinois. The coach at the time would always tell us players that practice does not make perfect. Instead, he would say that perfect practice makes perfect. I took those words to heart and was committed to every swing I took. I never took a swing or pitch for granted because each time was an opportunity to improve. This philosophy has served me well even into my adult years of life. I set out to achieve the goal of playing college and professionally and proved to myself that, with hard work and commitment, I could do anything I set my mind to. Often, when playing in college and the Minor Leagues, I would think back to those days of standing in the backyard and hitting that ball down a clothesline from tree to tree. It just goes to show you how powerful commitment can be when we dedicate ourselves completely to something.

LESSONS AND SUCCESS PRINCIPLES
Commitment vs. Interested

The word commitment gets tossed around easily without appreciating what it truly means. I define commitment as *doing what you said you would do long after the feeling and emotion of when you said it has passed.* For example, think back to a time when you were at a conference with a lot of people, great energy, and the perfect music that added to the excitement of the moment. The speaker on stage was delivering their keynote, and you could have sworn they were speaking directly to you. The message cut through to your core and gave you chills up your spine. At the end of the speech, you had a notebook full of notes, and you said to yourself, "This is it; this is my time." You were passionate during the speech and declared to yourself that you would not leave the event the same as you arrived. That is the emotion I am referring to. The true test of your commitment happens when you go home and back into your natural habitat and routine. The same environment that created bad habits is back to try and pull you into the familiar.

The question becomes, will you still be as committed and excited about your goal six months from now as you were at the time you said it? There is a honeymoon period many people experience. For a while, they are all-in on their commitment, but then life knocks them off course. Maybe it is hearing "no" for the first time, and it takes the wind out of their sails. Maybe they had the best intentions, but nothing fundamentally changed regarding their daily habits and schedule to support their commitment. The key to achieving success in life lies in our ability to stay committed.

What about the alternative? What does it mean if we commit to something but do not stick to it? The prime example we often use is the New Year's resolution. Every year, people wake up on January 1 and decide to set lofty goals for themselves. Whatever the goal, motivation often quickly fades because it was created in a state of emotion without fully acknowledging the full commitment and sacrifice it will take. This is better described as being "interested." The difference between being interested in a goal versus being committed to a goal is that it only sticks when things are convenient. When we are interested in a goal, it sounds good for a period because usually, it presents itself as easily attainable. When we are interested in a goal, there may be a path of least resistance we envision instead.

It is important to understand the difference between being committed versus being interested so we can ask ourselves in challenging moments which one of the two we truly are. Do we say yes because it sounds good but know deep down that distractions will likely throw us off course? Or does it speak to our soul and align with our Big Why, so we enthusiastically commit to it? When we are committed, we become borderline obsessed. To take it further, when we commit to something, it is really a measure of our character and integrity. If I asked you to define what integrity means to you, what would you say? It likely includes something along the lines of doing what you said you were going to do. That sounds familiar, doesn't it? Being a person of integrity is directly linked to commitment because it is doing what *we* said we would do, long after the feeling or emotion when we said it has passed. Our words matter. What we commit to matters.

How many times have we said yes to a party invitation, knowing full well we had no intention of going? We do this same thing to ourselves. We may say yes to something, but deep down, we know we will not do it. What this ends up developing is muscle memory. Just like lifting weights, we are getting repetitions in, and with enough repetitions, we end up developing muscle memory. How is it okay to build muscle memory of consistently breaking promises to ourselves, let alone others? Why are we conditioning ourselves to make promises we won't keep? I will go to the gym tomorrow. I will make my bed when I get up in the morning. I will make the call to have that conversation later. It is easy to say these things but many fail to act because their commitment was never genuine in the first place. Instead of building a commitment muscle that serves us, we are building the muscle memory of breaking promises, procrastination, and letting others down.

Next time we say we are going to do something, we must first pause for a moment. Are we really going to do it? Are we committed to fulfilling what we said we were going to do and upholding our integrity, or are we just interested in the momentary feeling and it's not that important to us? As I've said previously, if it is important to us, then we will find a way, and if not, then we will find an excuse.

Indecision Is the Thief of Opportunity

When I am coaching or speaking, I always make a point to highlight the word "decide." The reason is that many will prolong their success due to indecision. Indecision can be the thief of opportunity. Opportunity does not go away; it just goes to others willing to decide and capitalize on the moment. The success we desire is one decision away; our job is to simply make the decision. Let's take a deeper look. If you examine the word "decide," it has "cide" in it. Cide literally means to kill off. Consider other words with cide in them, such as pesticide and insecticide. In this context, when we speak about being committed and advancing boldly in the direction of our dreams, it requires us to decide. What does that mean we are killing off? In many cases, we are killing off doubt, complacency, procrastination, and mediocrity. It means we have a decided heart. Once and for all, we are going to take a stance for ourselves, dig our heels in, and proceed, knowing there will be obstacles and challenges we face, but the result is inevitable because we have decided. There is no alternative. We will do what it takes for as long as it takes to obtain the outcome we and our families deserve.

A lighthearted example of this is the squirrel. Yes, the squirrel. Depending on the personality type we even reference squirrels to explain why our attention span is so short and how distractions pop up and take our focus away from what we are trying to achieve. "Squirrel!" They are notorious daredevils that cross the road without much attention to traffic. Busy streets are lined with dead squirrels who could not decide. They went left, they went right, they went forward, and they went backward. They had no sense of direction about where they were going, so they ran aimlessly many times to their demise. How many of our goals and dreams lie alongside a road somewhere because we were unwilling to decide? How many goals and dreams have gotten trampled on by others because they were just lying there in the middle of the road? Our goals and success require us to be decisive. They will require us to kill off everything else.

In my own life, I have learned to be at peace when making decisions in several ways. One is knowing that no matter what I decide, there is no way everyone will be happy with my decision. Leadership can be lonely, and I am not trying to win any popularity contests. I simply focus on making the next right decision with the information I have at the time and take action that aligns with my values. I accept that not every decision will be popular, but popularity and doing what is right are two very different things. I can accept that I am responsible for my decisions and the consequences that come with them. I will make plenty of mistakes, but at least they are my mistakes that were rooted in good intentions with a decided heart. Andy Andrews says in the book *The Traveler's Gift*,[6] "My life will not be an apology. It will be a statement." We do not let others judge us by our results but rather by our intentions and knowing we made the decision that felt right in the moment. It is a statement of our character and commitment to doing what we felt was right.

In baseball, the best players who enter the Hall of Fame succeeded three out of ten times. Think about that. They earned millions of dollars yearly by succeeding three out of ten times. That means they failed seven out of ten. Clearly, those hitters did not make the right decision every time, nor did they come out successful every at-bat, but they continued to show up and take their swings. They gave themselves a chance to win. Undoubtedly, they swung at bad pitches, which was an unpopular decision. The crowd maybe even booed them for having an awful at-bat. There is no doubt they made baserunning mistakes and errors in the field when playing defense. Those were bad decisions too, but they were able to work through and continually show up. We are one decision away from having the success we desire. We can be anywhere we want to be within five years, so let's make the decision right now. The time is going to pass anyway, so why not utilize every day to get closer to our goals?

QUESTIONS TO CONSIDER:

1. In what area of my life do I need to decide right now?

2. On a scale of one to ten, how would I rank my commitment level right now?

3. When was I operating at a level ten commitment?

4. When was I operating at a level one commitment?

5. What have I been avoiding that needs my attention right now?

6. What do I need to say "no" to right now because my heart is truly interested, not committed?

7. What unfinished business do I need to revisit and see through to the finish line?

8. Am I playing to win or playing not to lose? What is the difference?

9. When is a time that indecision cost me an opportunity?

10. What would playing all-in look like to me right now?

STOP AND COMPLETE:

In this exercise, you are going to test your commitment level. It will be a measure of your willingness to become vulnerable and transparent. You can focus more than ever on your goal for the next ninety days or return to old habits. This exercise is a tool we do with every coaching client, and it is called the 90-Day Game Plan. Complete this exercise in the Cannonball Workbook, and then share it with someone who cares enough to hold you accountable and ask tough questions that will force you to defend the plan and your commitment.

To begin, the first section requires you to set a clear goal. Remember to set a S.M.A.R.T. goal with ninety days being the time frame. For example, your primary objective could be financial, physical, mental, etc., as long as it is specific, measurable, attainable, relevant, and time-stamped. Once you have your primary goal set for the next ninety days, you will continue to the three core pillars. What are the top three pillars you must complete to achieve one primary goal? Imagine one pillar represents one hundred percent of you achieving your goal. How can you build a plan clear enough to accomplish one hundred percent of the goal by itself without even needing the other two columns? Build each column as if one hundred percent of the goal could be achieved by it alone.

Conversely, if you only achieve thirty-three percent of the goal in each column, it still totals one hundred percent of the overall objective. And yet, what is great about this is if you knock it out of the park and accomplish one hundred percent of each pillar then you may be at three times your original goal. For example, if my goal is to sell five homes over the next ninety days in real estate, I may identify the first pillar to be open houses, the second to be networking events, and the third to be social media. This provides three different pillars I can create strategies around where all roads lead to the same desired outcome of selling five homes in the next ninety days.

Lastly, is the action items section. Underneath each pillar, you will be challenged to identify up to five action items for each. This is where the rubber meets the road. The five action items must still be specific, measurable, attainable, relevant, and time-stamped. Get as specific as possible because these represent the daily and weekly activities you must complete. These strategies should translate directly into your schedule, so your calendar serves as your accountability. To assist with this, I have provided an example and a blank template for you to complete. Commit, decide, and get to work.

CHAPTER 6

QUESTION EVERYTHING

"When you are a leader, your job is to have all the questions. You have to be incredibly comfortable looking like the dumbest person in the room. Every conversation you have about a decision, a proposal, or a piece of market information has to be filled with you saying, "What if?" and "Why not?" and "How come?"

JACK WELCH

HAVE FUN AND MAKE SURE YOU LISTEN!

In the summer of 2023, I dropped off our youngest daughter at a friend's house for a sleepover. The last words I told her were, "Have fun, and make sure you listen!" When I returned to my truck it got me thinking whether I was following my own advice. I thought about the everyday interactions I have with our daughters, and our youngest is notorious for asking the most random questions. Here are a few gems for you to get a laugh out of:

"Who is the oldest person in the world?"

"What are teeth made out of?"

"Who was the first person buried?"

"How much money do you have?"

"Do turtles die when it storms?"

"How was the world made?"

These highlight the genuine curiosity of a child and their innocence in wanting to learn and consume as much information as possible. I used that moment as an opportunity to reflect on myself. Do I still have that genuine curiosity? Am I asking enough questions? Am I too worried about being right that I have stopped being inquisitive?

In the book *A More Beautiful Question*,[7] the author Warren Berger cites that one estimate puts the number of questions a child asks between the ages of two and four years old is 40,000! That would mean that during the two-year span representing 730 days, a child would average nearly 55 questions per day. We have a lot to learn from children, especially regarding the art of asking questions. Their thirst for knowledge and demonstration of curiosity is one we should revisit rather than worrying about having the answers all the time.

THE CLASSIC RED FACE

Believe it or not, in high school, I was reserved and petrified of public speaking. I never liked standing up in front of the class to speak, let alone raising my hand to ask a question. I was the typical kid who sat near the back of the room and would never ask questions out of fear of looking or sounding silly to my peers. I got a C in speech class, and I am pretty sure the only reason I got a C to pass was because my teacher was my next-door neighbor. Kidding, not kidding! I would generally stand in front of the class with the paper covering my face and read directly from it so I could sit back down as soon as possible. Every time I was called on or forced to ask a question, my face would turn bright red out of embarrassment.

I believe my response then was from wanting to have all the answers. I saw asking questions as a weakness. I did not want to openly admit that I did not know something, so rather than asking questions to get the answer, I said nothing. I now realize this robbed me of being "learning-based," which would have allowed me to go further faster. I finally realized I had to break this terrible behavior when I served in leadership roles because my responsibility was not necessarily to have all the answers; in fact, my responsibility was to ask the best questions. I came to realize that asking questions was not a sign of weakness at all. It was a sign of intelligence, curiosity, and an open demonstration that I seek first to understand and do not have to have all the answers.

It all came together during a leadership training course I attended. A mentor of mine was sharing about his first year of real estate, and when he was asked the question by his first client, "Why should we hire you to be our real estate agent?" he responded brilliantly by stating, "The reason you should hire me is because I am a professional and let me explain what a professional means to me. A professional is someone who knows what they know, and they also know what they don't know, and they know the difference between the two. So when you hire me, you are getting a professional knowing that when you ask me a question, if I know the answer, I will tell you, and if I do not know the answer, I will also tell you that. However, if I do not know the answer, I will find out and get back to you."

Wow! That demonstration sums things up perfectly. We do not have to have all the answers. That is not our job. It is not seen as a weakness if we admit we do not know something. The real weakness is pretending that we know it all when we really do not because then, our ego is just getting in the way. Being learning-based and asking questions is what leads to ultimate success.

LESSONS AND SUCCESS PRINCIPLES
Who is in Control?

The person in control of a conversation asks the most questions. The person who is doing the most talking is doing the most bonding. This simple principle has served me well throughout my years of leadership and coaching. As someone with a lot to say, it is a reminder that I need to do less talking and more listening. After all, God gave us two ears and one mouth for a reason. All of this became abundantly clear to me in 2016, when I began my journey as a coach. I distinctly remember telling my coach how exhausted I was at the end of each day. After explaining how I felt, there was a long pause on the phone. The silence was interrupted by her asking me a simple question, "Jake, what is your question-to-statement ratio?" Confused by the question, I asked her to explain further what she meant. She proceeded to say that if I was truly coaching, then I should not be exhausted at the end of the day. The reason I was so tired was because I was doing all the talking. That is when it sank in, and I understood what she was getting at. Questioning my statement-to-question ratio was her saying I was talking too much. Like the 80/20 principle shared earlier, I was challenged only to speak twenty percent of the time and listen the other eighty. Besides, the one asking the most questions is the one who is in control of the conversation.

Early in my career, I fell back into the belief system thinking I had to have all the answers and over explain myself to other people. However, as Jack Welch preached, my job was not to have all the answers; it was to have the most questions so I could lead the other person through self-discovery. We are all whole, creative, and resourceful. It may not be new information we need; it may just be a reminder of things we already know but have not acted on. This reinforces the power of asking great questions.

I began to explore internally why so many of us feel the need to have answers and explain ourselves to show off how much we know. It led me down a road of personal growth where I came across this quote by Theodore Roosevelt, "People do not care how much you know until they know how much you care." That still did not answer my bigger question, so I swam upstream a little further, and here is the conclusion I came up with. During our early years of formal education, we were always incentivized to have all the right answers. We would study for standardized tests and be graded on pass or failure based upon how many we got right. Our intelligence was represented through a grade point average. We would work hard to get an A+ and stars on our homework. Every determiner of success was rooted in having the right answers.

Over time, this conditioning steers us away from asking questions, and it becomes solely about having the right answer. If we do not know the answer that means a red mark on the paper. By thinking through what programming causes myself and others to always want to be right, I could then understand the perspectives of others. I always believed that one of the quickest ways to success is by observing what the masses are doing and heading in the opposite direction. In this case, if most people were more concerned with being right and having all the answers, then clearly the opposite direction was not being worried about having all the answers and asking more questions. From that point forward, I committed to a quest of studying the art of asking great questions, and it has opened doors of opportunity for me ever since.

Who does not like to talk about themselves? Very few people. What I was able to figure out is, if I became more interested in someone else instead of being worried about how interesting I was, then I would be successful. How? People do business with those who they know, like, and trust. It is the trust factor that is the most difficult to achieve. It takes time to build trust, and yet, it can be lost in an instant. I began to connect the dots that the person who does the most talking means they are also doing the most bonding. I began to flip the script by asking questions twenty percent of the time and letting the other person speak the rest of the time. When I began to show genuine interest in their lives by giving them the space to talk, instant rapport and trust were established. It is the quickest hack to build trust with someone, and it all stems from our ability to ask questions, lead with curiosity, and always be learning-based.

The Art of Asking Questions

What makes questions so important? In leadership, our job is not to tell other people what to do. Our job is to help them self-discover what to do and become the author of their own actions and goals. A mentor of mine put it this way, leadership is "teaching people how to think the way they need to think, so they can do what they need to do when they need to do it, so they can get what they want when they want it."

Before we get to what a great question is, let's look at what a great question can do.

- It can allow us to listen deeply. Often, we are more concerned about responding and what we will say next to avoid any dreaded awkward silence. This means we were not actively listening. A best practice is to repeat what the person just said and ask another question from their answer, so you can drill down even deeper.

- We can unlock solutions never seen before. This is referred to as a pattern interruption. Our brains can be on autopilot much of the time, so when we ask a question, we interrupt the cycle, allowing the other person to see, hear, and feel outside of the initial boundaries of the discussion.

- It can expose areas of new awareness, growth, and learning. Questions take us out of the current state where our focus may be misaligned and enable us to see the bigger picture and scan the horizon.

- We can relate and get on their level. By seeking first to understand and coming from curiosity, we avoid judgment and can put ourselves in someone else's shoes. This will allow us to gain a different perspective and observe different things.

- It can allow us to go deeper into conversations to get to the heart of the matter. In an era of social media, we have become the least social in many ways. The art of asking questions and being able to communicate effectively depends on our ability to remain learning-based instead of having all the answers.

How do we know when we have asked a great question? Some may say the answer is the amount of silence between the moment we finish our question and when the other person responds. The failure many people make is not letting the silence do the heavy lifting. When you ask a great question, the other person will process. You will see their eyes shift, and when that happens, they are in a state of thought. Giving them the space to think is one of the most powerful gifts we could ever give someone. Unfortunately, many people will continue talking due to their own discomfort. They feel awkward when there is nothing but silence, so they continue talking. By doing this, we rob the other person of the opportunity to think and come up with their new realization.

What are other characteristics of powerful questions?

- They are open-ended rather than yes or no and allow the person to explore, wonder, and elaborate.

- They are short and simple. Some of the most powerful questions show up in the simplest forms. Long and drawn-out questions are usually a result of stacking multiple questions into one without giving the person an opportunity to respond, causing their thoughts to scatter. When we ask a question, it is important to let the other person finish their thoughts and wait a few seconds.

- They promote self-discovery. When we ask questions that give the other person an out-of-body type of experience, it removes them from the emotion of the situation and into a different space. Some examples would be, "What about this is important to you?" or "When this happens, what do you notice about yourself?" or "If your friend was going through something similar, what advice would you give them?"

- They allow for imagination and creativity. Great questions give permission to the other person to explore, dream, and wonder. They may discover their mindset is flawed or their actions need adjustment. Take the stance that every person is whole, creative, and resourceful. The answer lies within them already, we just need to ask the right questions and give them the space to think.

- They are not leading questions. We must be cautious that our questions are not a statement of our own with a question mark at the end. Leading questions steer the other person in the direction we want them to go. Our ability to remove ourselves from the situation and ask open-ended questions is no different than a young child asking questions because they are truly curious and do not know any better.

- They are growth-minded and solution-focused. We do not want to ask questions that only take people back into the state of once was. Our questions must also be focused on growth, opportunity, future, and solutions. There are amazing coaching models that facilitate a roadmap of growth for others that will be shared later in this chapter.

Let's take a moment and rank the quality of a question from lowest to highest. Previously, we discussed how not all activities are weighted equally with concepts such as the 80/20 Principle. Similarly, not all questions are weighted equally either. Through my experience and training, these are the various forms of questions we can ask from lowest quality to highest:

- Why? First, any question is better than no question at all. However, in the right context, questions that begin with the word "why" can be the lowest on the quality scale. Think back to a time in your life when you acted toward a goal and a friend asked you, "Why would you do that?" How did that make you feel? Many times, questions that begin with why provoke a knee jerk reaction from us rooted in defensiveness. When someone asks us why, it is tempting to go into justification and explanation mode. Of course, there is a time and place to ask questions rooted in why; however, things can take on an entirely new meaning if we adjust one word. For example, I could ask, "Why is that important to you?" or I could ask, "What about that is important to you?" I am essentially asking the same question, but I may get two very different responses.

- The next question on the quality scale would begin with "how." How questions are wonderful to ask, especially when seeking to obtain methods, tactics, or strategies. The area we must be mindful of is by asking, "How?" because it activates the logistical part of our minds. We go straight to tactics and solutions and possibly miss other factors that we need to examine. It is very easy for the doer personalities to fall into how-mode because their nature is to fix things and get into action. Given the context and scenario, these can be powerful questions to help people move forward, but be aware of the ramifications too.

- Next on the quality scale are "what" questions. Many leaders will use questions that begin with the word "what" quite often. This is an excellent skill, especially when we can use what instead of why or how. Throughout this book, many questions I ask begin with the word what. This is intentional because it opens your mind and possibilities.

- The highest quality of question begins with the word "who." The highest quality questions begin with who because they allow us to gain perspective. It reminds us that no one succeeds alone, and others have walked before us. It may result in finding a coach or mentor. Who questions may lead us to shadow someone for a day that we have identified. Who questions also bring us to a place of leverage where we realize someone else can do a better job than us. Who questions are what business owners have learned to master because they cannot do it all themselves. They ask who, rather than why, how, or what. Any challenge or new phase of growth can be resolved by a relationship. We can ask who can help, rather than panicking and wondering what we should *do*.

The topic of asking great questions is a large one to tackle, but I am highlighting its importance, as well as understanding the difference between a good question and a great one. Keep in mind, the person who is asking the most questions is in control of the conversation, which means the person doing the most talking is doing the most bonding. Allow them to build trust with you and show a genuine interest, and you will be amazed at the doors of opportunity that open.

QUESTIONS TO CONSIDER:

1. How can I take what I just learned and apply it?
2. What question do I need to ask myself, using "Who" as the beginning?
3. What question do I need to ask myself using "What" as the beginning?
4. What area of my life can I identify where I need to ask more questions?
5. What is my question-to-statement ratio during a typical conversation?
6. Where am I more focused on being right than asking questions to learn?
7. Who is someone I can think of who excels at asking great questions?
8. What is a question someone has asked me that really impacted me?
9. How have questions helped shape my decisions?
10. What steps can I take to improve at asking questions?

STOP AND COMPLETE:

In my early years of becoming intentional regarding asking better questions, my coach gave me an exercise that was tremendously helpful, and I am going to pass it along to you. The challenge was to write down fifty questions every week and turn them in to her.

Initially, I was intimidated by this challenge, so I reluctantly agreed. In my mind, fifty questions were a lot, and it would take me hours every week to do this.

Contrary to my belief, it was incredibly fun, productive, enlightening, and efficient. She gave me a tip to open a business book and read a couple of pages. However, instead of reading it for the information, she told me to read it through a different lens. The lens was to question everything and see how each sentence could prompt a question. I found this to be very effective, and for every question I came up with, I could think of multiple questions from it. I could think of various other ways to ask the question. Before I knew it, I had fifty questions, and it took me no more than fifteen to twenty minutes to complete.

My challenge for you is the same. Pick a topic or read a few pages of a book like my coach suggested and come up with fifty questions on your own and write them down in your Cannonball Workbook. Any question counts, but if you want to level up, be cognizant of the quality of questions you come up with. How many of them begin with the words why, what, how, or who? This is a powerful exercise to condition your mind to think in the form of questions, rather than always thinking in the form of answers.

CHAPTER 7

CLEAN YOUR ROOM, OR ELSE!

"Being held accountable is an act of generosity and compassion. It is a gift that someone gives us to correct our wrongs, unlearn, and do better for the sake of our own growth. It might be uncomfortable, but it is worth the discomfort."

MINAA B.

OH, HOW THE TABLES CAN TURN

"Go pick up your room before you go out and play."

"Make sure you bring socks downstairs with you."

"Grab your cleats and soccer bag and put it in the car."

The list continues with common phrases my wife and I have said to our kids. As a parent, one of our greatest duties is to teach responsibility and accountability to our children. Parenting styles might differ from one household to another, yet the underlying principle is teaching them respect and integrity. We are preparing them for adult life and to be responsible for their actions. It is funny when the kids turn the tables on you as the parent. The fight is not even fair! There have been times I would think our daughters are the adults in the equation when teaching me accountability.

For example, one summer, we created a weekly checklist of responsibilities for both girls. The checklist had everything from reading a book to picking up their rooms to filling up the dog's water bowl. If they had checked all the boxes on their weekly checklist for all of the weeks of the summer, then we agreed we would take them on a vacation to Turks and Caicos. I know what you are thinking: *that is quite a big reward for doing basic tasks on a checklist*, but my wife and I were planning on booking that dream vacation anyway. We thought it might be fun to tie it to their responsibilities and incentivize them with some accountability.

By the end of the summer, the girls had done an incredible job. Maybe it wasn't perfect, but they really took it seriously and earned the big reward. As time went on, they continually asked if we had booked the trip yet. "Did you book it yet? When are we going?" It got me thinking that our children can be the absolute best accountability partners in the world. If we want to be held accountable, tell a child what the intentions are, and they will ask every single day until we cannot handle it anymore. The same was true for me. Left up to me and my chaotic schedule, I may have continued to delay and procrastinate, but thanks to my children, who flipped the script and held me accountable, I took action and was forced to book the vacation with them looking over my shoulder every step of the way. It is amazing what will happen when we insert accountability into our lives.

WRITE THE BOOK ALREADY!

At the time of writing this, it had been eight years since I had the inspiration to write. For eight consecutive years, I wrote in my yearly letter to myself that I was going to write this book. I have had the title picked out since day one. My business LLC even has the name Cannonball in it. Year after year, I would cringe when I read the previous year's letter because I said I would write the book and never got around to it. The sequence was painful because each year, I swore this would be the one, only to open the letter the following year and read the empty promise again. I finally decided to take my own advice, and with the help of my peers holding me accountable, I committed to a deadline and created a S.M.A.R.T. goal. Knowing myself, I booked a rental home for one week so I could isolate myself from the world and do nothing but write. As I type, I am in that very rental home that looks out over the beautiful Wisconsin River.

Without accountability to others and going public with my goal to write this book once and for all, it would have likely kept getting pushed off down the road. Everything happens for a reason, and the timing is not coincidental. Had I written the book any earlier, I am not sure I would have the wisdom and experiences my children have given me. Over the years, I would email myself lessons and principles that our children were teaching me so I could save them for this day. Whatever you may be putting off right now, I would encourage you to take accountability and decide to get it done.

LESSONS AND SUCCESS PRINCIPLES
The Buck Stops with You

When we hear the word accountability, what comes to mind? For years I would think of accountability as micromanagement. I would cringe at the idea of accountability because I value my autonomy and freedom at an extremely high level. During my early years of being an entrepreneur, I would always scoff at the idea of needing someone to hold me accountable. I saw myself as driven, a self-starter, and very disciplined. On top of that, why would I have someone basically act as my "boss" when I just left corporate America and wanted to be in business for myself? My stubbornness finally caught up to me when I struggled financially and submersed myself into personal growth.

What I came to realize was that if I wanted things to change, then I had to change. I had to revisit my programming on what accountability meant to me. All high achievers sprint towards accountability. I read author after author, who said things like "No one succeeds alone." If I wanted to get serious about pursuing my version of success, then I had to adopt a high degree of accountability in my life. I have always valued consistency and never asked people to do something I wouldn't do myself or at least wouldn't be willing to do. I refused to continue operating as a fraud, so I reprogrammed my belief system around accountability. Rather than seeing it as micromanagement, I realized it is a form of love. It was someone who cared enough about me to call me out on things when I was not behaving in a way that aligned with my values and goals. Accountability was someone else holding me able because when left to my own vices, I was my own worst accountability partner. It was too easy to let myself off the hook. I was creating a habit of arguing more for my limitations than standing up for what I wanted.

When I hired my first official business coach in 2016, it changed my life forever. With the help of my coach, she provided accountability that kept my actions and goals on track. This allowed me to develop The Locker Room and become the number one coaching program within the first six months for the largest real estate company in the world at the time. I had the ideas and strategies and knew exactly what I wanted to achieve. I was off to the races, but many times, growth can be messy, and the next thing I knew, I looked up and didn't even recognize where I was anymore.

Think of it this way: imagine you are taking your family on a vacation across the country for a fun road trip. As soon as you sit down in the car, you likely turn on your GPS for directions from where you are to where you desire to be. No path is perfect, so about two hours into the trip, you encounter road construction and must take a detour. Immediately, your GPS recalculates a new route. It shows you every turn to make and even gives you the option of multiple roads you can take that all end up at the desired location. In essence, your GPS became your accountability partner. You knew exactly what you wanted, but how you would get there changed because the road was under construction, and you were forced to go a different way. The result did not change because things did not go as planned; you just found a new way. This is exactly how accountability towards our goals can work in life too.

Growth is messy. The journey is never going to be perfect. You may have to reinvent yourself and your plan multiple times. However, if you know exactly where you desire to end up and why you are going there in the first place, then the destiny is assured. The path may not be clear, and you may get inconvenienced switching routes along the way, but if you keep the focus on the end destination, then nothing else matters. Instead of the trip taking fifteen hours, maybe it took twenty. At least you made it! Your goals may take you longer than expected, but if you keep going, does it really matter as long as you eventually get there?

What comes with being accountable and accepting that the buck stops with you? Let's examine a few key areas you must recognize to be accountable.

- Extreme ownership. In his book *Extreme Ownership*,[8] Jocko Willink, former Navy Seal, wrote: "Leaders must own everything in their world. There is no one else to blame. When setting expectations, no matter what has been said or written, if substandard performance is accepted and no one is held accountable—if there are no consequences—that poor performance becomes the new standard." George Bernard Shaw wrote, "People are always blaming their circumstances for what they are. I don't believe in circumstances. The people who get on in this world are the people who get up and look for the circumstances they want, and if they can't find them, make them."

There is no shortage of powerful and inspiring quotes from high achievers on accountability. The trend we will see emerge consistently is the resistance to blaming others. Our success, failure, actions, and attitude are wholly owned by us and no one else. Accountability requires us to come to grips with extreme ownership. We can no longer hide behind others or circumstances. We must accept a new level of responsibility and transparency that comes with being a person of high accountability.

- No victim mindset. Accountability requires us to focus on solutions. Deepak Chopra said, "When you blame and criticize others, you are avoiding some truth about yourself." We must look in the mirror and question where our DNA is regarding any success or failure. It is easy to go down the road of a victim mindset and constantly question, "Why me?" or "I knew I was going to fail at this." A victim mindset has no place in someone's world when they embrace full accountability.

- Life doesn't happen to you; life happens for you. As Paulo Coelho said, "It's always easy to blame others. You can spend your entire life blaming the world, but your success and failures are entirely your own responsibility." I am not numb to the fact that we all go through some hardships. I have never met a high achiever who hasn't. It is part of life and being human that we find ourselves in tough situations. But those who can see the forest from the trees will stand to win because they are willing to take back control and be accountable. Next time we go through something difficult, we can pause and ask, "How will this positively serve me in the future?" Every great challenge also carries a lesson, and it is our job to extract the gift inside that moment. What do we stand to learn?

- Transparency. Being accountable requires a high degree of transparency. We can no longer hide in the bushes and be an observer of life watching it pass us by at high rates of speed. We must actively participate and take control of our minds, actions, and results. Transparency forces us to step out. We all entered this world naked, afraid, and full of life. Leveraging transparency allows the world to see the real us. It reveals a new level of vulnerability and authenticity because we are standing strong in faith that we are the one who gets to design our lives. As Andy Andrews says in *The Traveler's Gift*,[9] "When faced with a decision, many people say they are waiting for God. But I understand, in most cases, God is waiting for me."

The Benefits: Accountability and Visibility

"I am not a product of my circumstances.
I am a product of my decisions."

STEVEN COVEY

When we take full ownership and embrace accountability, we immediately propel ourselves forward toward the direction of our dreams. Tony Robbins reminds us of the benefits of taking action supported by accountability by saying, "Change happens when the pain of staying the same is greater than the pain of change." Deep down, we may be resisting accountability due to a fear of change. Change requires us to be open-minded. It requires us to be vulnerable again. Change forces us to go from the familiar into the unfamiliar. It demands that we become students again and accept that we still have much to learn. Any time we do something for the first time, we traditionally are not very good at it. However, the more we do something, it becomes a habit, and then eventually, it becomes involuntary and we do not even have to think about it.

When teaching our daughters to ride a bike, it was always a test of will and patience. They had to get on the bike, fall off, and experience some bumps and bruises along the way. And yet, with repetition and willingness to adapt, they eventually caught on, and the next thing we knew, they were zipping up and down the driveway like it was second nature. This is no different than what we may do every day when we head to work. It is the same routine of getting into the car, starting up the engine, and making our way into the office. We likely did not even have to think of which street to turn on. We were on autopilot as our mind wandered off, thinking about the game last night. Many times, we may not even realize how we got there; we just did it without thinking.

When we embrace change, it requires us to recalibrate and be held accountable to a new set of actions. Holding ourselves to this new standard and sharing it with others can have many benefits for our relationships as well. The visibility of our actions plays an important role in our accountability. When we share with a friend or loved one what our intentions are, they are now watching to see what we do. Are we committed? Are we a person of integrity? Assuming the answer is yes, this can result in a higher level of trust, dependability, and more opportunity.

Let's talk about lessons from a lemonade stand to further illustrate the importance of visibility. Visibility is directly linked to income generating business activities as well. Imagine for a moment that we are driving down the road, and we see a young child with a lemonade stand. Pause for a moment and think about what was just witnessed. A young child is running their own business. They are being entrepreneurial. The child did not hope to sell lemonade by sitting inside their home and praying for people to knock on the door and come to them. Instead, the young entrepreneur is highly visible on the side of the road and boldly claims, "Here I am! I am open for business!" They likely placed themselves in a high-traffic area and have no shame putting themselves out there for the best visibility. Rather than waiting back for people to come to them, they likely have signs, balloons, and a table while frantically waving their arms to encourage others to stop and buy lemonade from them. What can we learn from this? How does this translate into our pursuit of success? Are we putting ourselves out there to be highly visible, or are we expecting people to find us by luck or some other passive force?

We spoke earlier about trust. Trust can be obtained by asking questions and listening to others. Another level of establishing trust boils down to accountability and visibility. When we do what we said we would do, and others have the opportunity to observe our behaviors, they see that we are a person of our word. The walls of skepticism break because they trust that we have character and will follow through not just with our words but with actions. Remember the phrase, "Actions speak louder than words"? When we demonstrate that we are accountable through action, others begin to trust us, and with trust comes a deeper relationship. As a business owner, one can see that the team will play harder for the owner with character. They will proactively seek to take on more work. They will develop a stronger bond to the company culture and the mission. Everything rises and falls on leadership, but I would add that everything rises and falls on accountable leadership.

Once trust is established then it leads to an enhanced feeling of dependability. Others will go out of their way to advocate for us because we have shown them we are trustworthy and dependable. I have built multiple businesses, and each has been successful in its own right. As a leader, I have had some of the biggest ideas and have put them into action. I have also failed, a lot. Some may say I have accelerated my learning by failing quicker and more often than others. Without a foundation of trust through accountability, there would be a revolving door of people leaving the company because they may believe I am just a guy who throws spaghetti against a wall. Yet, that has never been the case. I have built some of the strongest cultures within very large international companies that have gotten me on stage and highlighted by the owners of these companies. I have learned that through accountability and visibility, my team is able to see that I walk the walk. They witness me being in the trenches with them. They know I am working hard and constantly experimenting to find the next breakthrough. Without trust through accountability, there would be no dependability. My team depends on me to make messes and then clean them up. My team knows I have made many emotional deposits into their account, and occasionally, I need to make a withdrawal and ask for forgiveness. Because I am accountable, they may disagree with certain decisions or business ideas, but they can never question my integrity. When I say I am going to do something, I do it.

Another benefit of accountability that is worth noting is opportunity. Opportunity has always been a buzzword that attracts me like a moth to a light. If we were out to dinner and someone five tables over said the word opportunity, my head would immediately turn on a swivel. Who isn't looking for new and exciting opportunities to come their way? Being accountable affords us opportunities that we would have otherwise never dreamed of. Let's take inventory right now. We declared our goals and intentions, and we inserted accountability to monitor our actions; by following those actions, we have now built trust, and with that trust, we are more dependable than ever before. The natural progression is where all roads lead to more opportunities. Those opportunities may show up from our leadership if we are employed. Those opportunities may show up with strong affiliates and alliances through our network if we are self-employed. Whatever the case, opportunities have a magical way of presenting themselves when we take consistent and accountable actions. We do not have to get things right all the time; it is more important that we do the right thing all the time. This entire recipe creates a formula for success, and it is all controlled through us having extreme ownership of our actions and believing that if it is meant to be then it is up to me.

Character vs. Reputation

"Be more concerned with your character than your reputation. Character is what you really are. Reputation is what people say you are. Reputation is often based on character – but not always."

JOHN WOODEN

Accountability directly leads to building your character. July 4, 2006, was the last baseball game I ever pitched. I was in the Minor League system for the Anaheim Angels organization, playing in Idaho Falls, Idaho. Two years prior, I had reconstructive surgery on my pitching elbow and always promised myself I would never get a second surgery if I reinjured my pitching arm. During the game, I felt the familiar pain all over again. I could not believe it. Coach walked out of the dugout and took me out of the game because he could tell something was not right, and frankly, I was all over the place. I walked back to the dugout with my head down knowing what had just happened because I felt it before, but I did not say anything at the time to my coach. After the game, the bus took us back to our hotel. I had always observed that our coach was the last one to get off the bus, so I sat there, letting all of my teammates get off before me. The last one on, I walked up to coach and said, "Coach, can I talk to you for a second?" He immediately looked up, paused, and asked me, "It is your arm, isn't it?" I broke down in tears, and he assured me that we would speak tomorrow after I was able to regroup myself. I distinctly remember sitting outside of the hotel in a corner, curled up in the fetal position with my head in between my knees. It was over. This was a hard lesson in character building for me because, in an instant, it was all over. I was not going to go through another surgery, and it was time to move on with my life. Later, I became bitter and resentful toward the game because all my life, I had worked so hard, and just like that, it was over. I went through an identity crisis, wondering what I was going to do next. I ran through all the people in my mind that I felt like I was disappointing, being unable to play any further.

Eventually, what I realized was so profound and liberated me from those chains of negativity. I realized that I had confused performance with my identity. Performance is what we *do*. Identity is who we *are*. Let me repeat that. Performance is what we do, and identity is who we are. Just because I could not play baseball any longer does not mean I was lost. The lessons and principles baseball taught me have stuck with me no matter what I did next. In an instant, I was able to go from being resentful to joyful. I became aware of the fact that I was accountable for my own actions and how I chose to respond to the situation. When I no longer played the role of victim and instead played the role of victor, I became empowered to do great things, knowing I had so much I could apply to my future opportunities.

The same may apply to all of us. Where in our lives have we been able to overcome adversity and realize we are in control of our own destinies? Where have we realized that we are not the victim of a circumstance but rather the victor? Accountability builds character. Our character is going to be tested every single day. Some may describe character as what we do when no one is watching. When we say we are going to work but end up scrolling through social media instead, or when we say we are going to the gym but decide to hit the snooze button with the rationale that no one is watching, it speaks to our true character. One thing about character and how it applies to success is that success happens in the moment of decision. If I win the decision at the moment, then I will win the day. If I win the day, then I will win the week. If I win the week, then I will win the month. If I win the month, then I will win the quarter. If I win the quarter, then I will win the year. Success stems from the moment of decision. Often, it can seem insignificant. Yet our decisions shape us. In the words of Andy Andrews, "First we make a choice. Then our choices make us."

Building character through accountability is on display all around us. We used Olympic athletes as an example previously. This time, pay extra attention to what an Olympic sprinter does at the end of the race. Often, those races are won or lost by fractions of a second. These athletes have dedicated their entire lives to running for ten seconds every four years. Just imagine that. The stakes are high, and they are playing to win because they understand they are not just representing themselves; they are representing their entire country. Think about the character that builds in a person. If we watch those races closely, we will see every runner lean in just a little bit as they cross the finish line. Why would they do that? For those in front they do that to take every inch they can get to win the race, set a world record, or place in the medal standings. But what about the others? What about the athlete who knows they are not going to break any records, they are not going to break their personal best, but they still choose to sprint through the finish line and lean in? They understand it is a moment to build character and represent something so much greater than just themselves. They recognize it is not just about winning a medal, but the character they built along the way. The material items will come and go, but character sticks with us.

This may be your time to strengthen your character. This may be your moment to be the voice rather than the echo from everyone else's noisy opinion or walk in the shadows of others because you are timid to step out in faith. Let your character give you your voice back. You do not have to turn down your ambitions just because someone else thinks the volume is too loud. Cut through the noise, drown out the distractions, and get loud. Your future self is thanking you right now for taking a stance.

QUESTIONS TO CONSIDER:

1. What area of my life do I need accountability in right now?
2. Who do I respect and trust enough to hold me accountable?
3. What does accountability mean to me?
4. What are some methods someone could hold me accountable without creating resentment?
5. How has accountability served me well in the past?
6. What words would best describe my character?

7. What words would my top five closest people use to describe me?

8. What part of my life needs higher visibility and transparency to others?

9. What mindset shift do I need to welcome accountability into my life?

10. Why should higher accountability and visibility excite me?

STOP AND COMPLETE:

At various events presented by The Locker Room, one of my mentors, Kit Fucile, does an exercise where she encourages us to text five people on the spot. She pauses and has everyone take out their cell phones to text the top five people they are closest to. I will have you do the same exercise because the impact can be profound. You are going to text the top five people you associate with the most and say, *"I know this may be random, but it would really mean a lot to me if you would help me out with something. What words would you use to describe me?"* Write their responses down in your Cannonball Workbook.

The goal here is for them to respond with words or short phrases that they would use to describe you as a person. It is amazing to see the responses you will get. What traditionally happens are two things:

1. Patterns—You may observe a pattern emerging from similar responses.

2. The Mirror—You may see some responses and say, "Really?"

It is not uncommon to hear how others see you and then question whether you see yourself the same way. It is an amazing glimpse into the perception of others and the perception you have of yourself. It is important to accept their responses. Be sure to thank them and be willing to accept all the nice things people say about you. A gift you can give them in return is to repeat the exercise and list the complimentary words you would use to describe them as well.

CHAPTER 8

KNOW THE GAME

"Success is neither magical nor mysterious. Success is the natural consequence of consistently applying the basic fundamentals."

JIM ROHN

SEEING THE BEST IN THE WORLD

In 2023, my wife and I took our two daughters to the Core Hydration Classic in Hoffman Estates, Illinois. This was the first gymnastics meet that Simone Biles had competed in since the Tokyo Olympics in 2021. Our youngest daughter was obsessed with gymnastics and quite talented at her young age. The opportunity to see, arguably, the best gymnast ever was a once-in-a-lifetime experience. We had great seats next to the floor routine mat and showed up plenty early to see Simone Biles and all the gymnasts warm up. It was clear how fundamentally sound Simone Biles was compared to everyone else, not to mention her superior athleticism. During warmups, she would focus on all the little details. She would go at full speed as if she were being scored by the judges. You could just tell she went about everything a little bit differently than everyone else. Our youngest daughter was starstruck watching her compete.

Leading up to the competition, our daughter was competing in gymnastics meets during the winter months, and when she was not competing, she would practice one or two times per week. After seeing Simone Biles, something was triggered inside of our daughter. When we returned home, she immediately went upstairs, where she had a youth-sized set of tumbling bars in her room. She practiced on them for hours. She would also go downstairs in our living room, where we had a bouncy tumble track, and she would do cartwheels and other skills nonstop. It even got to the point where my wife and I had to play pretend and act as judges while scoring our daughter on creative routines that she had come up with. It was so fun to watch, and I could not help but pause and think of the influence watching Simone Biles had on her. Our daughter tried to replicate everything she had just seen one of her role models perform in person. When she was not physically moving, she would watch videos of girls' gymnastics.

All of this helped me realize that no matter what age or skill level we compete in, the fundamentals are what matter most. Simone Biles did not become the best in the world on sheer luck or talent alone. She was able to master the fundamentals of playing a sport at the highest level out of anyone else in the world. Seeing this helped me reflect on my own life and whether I was playing the "game" the right way. It forced me to slow down and remember that simplicity is what scales in business. It is tempting for me to get overly creative and lose sight of the fundamentals, but when we can master the fundamentals, it allows our creativity and natural skills to shine even brighter.

START BY PUTTING THE BALL ON A TEE

From late 2009 through 2012, I owned and operated an indoor baseball and softball training facility called The Player's Edge. This was my first endeavor into entrepreneurship, and I would give private lessons to young players, conduct camps and clinics, and even do video analysis breakdowns. During that time, I helped hundreds of players master game fundamentals through drills and one-on-one training. After a few years of doing this, something became abundantly clear to me that I have taken and applied successfully in my businesses. The basics of the game do not change; the game just speeds up. I taught the kids how to properly grip a baseball as a pitcher or how to properly hold the bat when they were batting. I made a point of telling them how the Major League Players they watch on television were literally doing the exact same thing. It does not matter if you are a kid playing Little League or earning millions of dollars every year in the majors; the game does not change; it just speeds up.

For example, when a young baseball player is in Little League, the pitcher may throw sixty m.p.h. And yet, they are holding the baseball with the exact same grip and using the same mechanics as the Major League player throwing at ninety-five m.p.h. The game did not change, the game just sped up. I was able to apply this in business for myself as well as those I have coached over the years. When working with a new real estate agent, I emphasize this point and show them how the blocking and tackling of this business does not change. The same fundamentals it takes to sell twelve homes per year are the same fundamentals it takes to sell 112. The game itself did not change; it just sped up.

I remember watching the Major League Baseball Home Run Derby during the All-Star break a few years ago. I will never forget the camera showed one of the participants in the middle of the Home Run Derby down in the batting cage and hitting a baseball off a tee. This same player is the one who went on to win the entire Home Run Derby that year. At that moment, I was struck because there was a player who could hit the ball five hundred feet, and he was in the middle of a Home Run Derby and was still working on the fundamentals in a batting cage. He was placing a ball on a tee and perfecting his swing. He could have thrown all his mechanics out the window and been tempted to get creative by dropping his back shoulder trying to lift the ball, but instead, he was working on taking quality swings and using proper fundamentals. We have much to learn by knowing the game and focusing on the fundamentals. At times, creativity can stunt our success. Preparing for success can be boring, mundane, and repetitious, but never forget that if it is good enough for a Major League player who earns millions of dollars per year to hit a ball off a tee, then nothing is too fundamental for us either.

LESSONS AND SUCCESS PRINCIPLES
Follow the Breadcrumbs

Tony Robbins said, "Success leaves clues. People who succeed at the highest level are doing something differently than everyone else does." It needs no validation, but Tony is correct. Whether it is business, playing an instrument, sports, or any other area of life, we can turn to those who have gone before us and learn about what they do that makes them different from everyone else. Previously, we spoke about studying the "game film," and it applies here too. Our ability to slow down and learn from others can catapult our success quicker than anything else. Similarly, Roy Williams said, "A smart man makes a mistake, learns from it, and never makes that mistake again. But a wise man finds a smart man and learns from him how to avoid the mistake altogether."

Consider an example most people can relate to. Imagine your best friend has a birthday coming up, and you want to bake them a delicious cake. Assuming you are not a professional chef, you do what most people resort to which is go to the grocery store and find the aisle with all the cake mixes. You stand there with your arms crossed until you spot the perfect cake you want to make for your friend. You grab the box off the shelf, study the picture on the front of it, and grab all the other ingredients it says you will need for the cake before heading to checkout. When you get home to bake the cake, you turn the box around and go step by step, following the instructions provided to you. If you do not set the oven at the proper temperature, make the proper measurements, or follow the proper sequence, the cake will not turn out right. The lesson here is that success requires us to be great at following a proven system that can create predictable results. It goes back to mastering the fundamentals. There is nothing exciting about mixing ingredients together and following directions, but what is exceptionally fun is when the end product is exactly what we envisioned. Just like the cake mix, there are recipes for success that we can learn from as well if we are just willing to follow directions.

Many people want what is on the front of the box without following the instructions on the back. For a business owner, it is easy for them to say they want to earn $250,000 per year. But do they have the recipe for success? Do they have step-by-step action plans to follow? Did they take the time to learn from others who have gone before them to see what ingredients they used? When we apply creativity before systems and models, we are gambling with the intended result. Creativity has its place, but only when we build things on a solid foundation first. Success can be boring and repetitious, just like putting the ball on the tee, but when there is a proven track record or system to follow, would we be willing to trade creativity for results? Simplicity is what can scale our success. When we overcomplicate things, it stunts our growth. Simplicity scales and complexity fails. If we are expected to do our research and follow the breadcrumbs left by others before us, then where do we start? What questions should we be asking?

Here are some questions that have helped me. Some of these questions are influenced by one of my favorite books by authors W. Chan Kim and Renee Mauborgne called *The Blue Ocean Strategy.*[10]

1. What business or market space am I in (or would like to be)?

2. What current industry trends do I observe?

3. What standards need to be raised in my industry?

4. What has never been offered before in my industry?

5. What areas are most companies competing against each other in?

6. What current assumptions am I operating within that need to be questioned or challenged?

7. What am I currently copying only because I feel it is necessary to remain competitive?

8. What is the greatest challenge I provide a solution for?

9. What solution do I provide for the greatest challenge people have?

10. Who is my ideal customer?

11. How can I create world-class experiences for my customers, so they become raving fans?

12. What can I implement that would make my competition irrelevant?

When doing our research and benchmarking others, these are some great questions we can ask ourselves. While others are playing checkers, we can play chess and be more strategic with our thinking. An example from my life was in early 2016 when I initially began formulating the vision of The Locker Room Real Estate Coaching and Training company. In Chapter 2, I discussed the Question Mind exercise, but something I did not mention was that I did this exercise for myself before The Locker Room was even a business. I could clearly see what I wanted to achieve, and yet, I knew I must slow down to consider all the angles and probabilities that would try to get in the way. I created a document that I still have with six pages full of questions I was asking. I did not pause to seek the answers; I asked every question I could think of. This way, I knew I was thinking strategically and covering all my bases. I could have rushed into action, but I was willing to slow down on the front end in order to speed up on the back end. That single exercise is the very reason I am still in business today. I knew if we were going to pull things off, it would take threading a very fine needle and playing our cards just right. It allowed me to play chess while others were playing checkers. For every challenge or question I received, I had already been there in my mind and was not taken by surprise.

Imagine, basketball player Michael Jordan sinking that game-winning shot as the clock turns over to 0:00 time left. The ball leaves his fingertips just as the clock runs out of time, and the crowd goes wild as the ball goes through the net. At that moment, the crowd is screaming, and the pressure of the situation is felt in the entire arena. But do you notice what happens after the game and the celebration is over? Jordan would get interviewed, and the host would ask, "How did you do it? What were you feeling?" and generally the greats like Jordan respond with something like, "I was calm. I wanted the ball in my hands. In my head, I have been in that exact situation ten thousand times already."

Did you catch that? Great players can slow the game down when the world around them is in chaos. They have visualized that moment ten thousand times already in practice and their visualization exercises. They can block out the noise and trust their skills. To be successful in business it is no different than what Michael Jordan and others go through. We must know what game we are playing and be ready for any situation. We must want the ball in our hands when the pressure is at its highest. We must be able to slow things down when everyone else is in chaos. What game are you playing? Are you following a formula for success to achieve what is on the front of the box? Do you have proven systems and models to guide you or are you in constant creativity? Have you taken the time to study what high achievers do? What questions do you need to ask so you are playing chess, not checkers?

Time to Put on Your "Fitbit" For Success

When establishing my game plan for the growth of The Locker Room, I applied everything I have shared thus far. I positioned myself with the highest percentage of success prior to taking action because I took the time to study, benchmark, and speak with others who had achieved the level of success I desired. Out of my experience, I was able to document the entire journey and create a course I have taught since 2017 called "The 13 Steps to Build a Scalable Business," which has helped countless entrepreneurs become successful. It provides a roadmap, a system to follow that allows you to insert creativity on top of it. Consider these steps the instructions on the cake mix box and your creativity can be the sprinkles that go on top.

Let's briefly examine each of the thirteen steps, but before we do, it is important to note that these are in a specific order. Failure to follow them messes up the entire recipe. All I can do is share with you what has worked for me, and what you choose to do with it is up to you. Additionally, without the full context of my teaching the material, I have given you the steps and additional questions or instructions underneath to assist in each concept.

Step 1: Research Your Opportunity

(These are the same set of questions provided earlier. It is not an exhaustive list; it is designed to help you get started.)

1. What business or market space am I in (or would like to be)?

2. What current industry trends do I observe?

3. What standards need to be raised in my industry?

4. What has never been offered before in my industry?

5. What areas are most companies competing against each other in?

6. What current assumptions am I operating within that need to be questioned or challenged?

7. What am I currently copying only because I feel it is necessary to remain competitive?

8. What is the greatest challenge that I provide a solution for?

9. What solution do I provide for the greatest challenge people have?

10. Who is my ideal customer?

11. How can I create world-class experiences for my customers, so they become raving fans?

12. What can I implement that would make my competition irrelevant?

Step 2: Establish Your Value Proposition

1. What is going to attract others to me?

2. Who do I connect with the most that I desire to serve?

3. What relevant experience or expertise do I bring that can help them?

    a. What problem do I solve?

4. Who is my ideal client?

    a. Is there a specific person who resembles my ideal client?

    b. What is it about that person that makes me enjoy working with them?

    c. What is their personality like?

    d. What value do they place on relationships?

    e. What do they do for fun?

    f. What other demographics would represent my ideal customer?

g. Is there a particular niche, location, or specialization to consider?

h. Where do they spend time outside of work?

i. What do they listen to or what do they read?

Step 3: Define Your Mission, Core Values, and Belief System

1. Mission Statement: What is my purpose? Why am I in business?

    a. A simple formula to help write a mission statement is the following: My mission is to _____ by/ through _____ so that _____.

    b. The first blank space represents my intention. (The What)

    c. The second blank space represents my method. (The How)

    d. The third blank space represents my desired outcome or bold promise (The Result)

2. Core Values

    a. What is important to me?

    b. What is the "why" behind my business?

    c. What are my priorities?

    d. What are the non-negotiables?

    e. What are the rules and guidelines that I follow?

3. Belief System

    a. What are the guiding beliefs that I live by?

   b.   What are my unwavering beliefs?

   c.   What am I willing to fight for?

Simon Sinek said it best when he said, "The goal is not to do business with everybody who needs what you have. The goal is to do business with people who believe what you believe."

Step 4: Build Your Product or Services Ecosystem

1. What product(s) am I going to offer?

2. What service(s) am I going to offer?

3. How much will they cost?

4. Is there a frequency to consider?

5. What is the commitment from the customer?

6. What is the value stack for each product or service?

Step 5: Build a Pro Forma for Your Business

1. What revenue do I expect to generate each month?

2. Is there seasonality to consider?

3. What percentage of growth do I expect month over month?

4. What are my fixed expenses?

5. What is my cost of sales?

6. What is the breakeven point for my business?

7. When do I expect to become profitable?

8. What am I going to pay myself?

Step 6: Build a Six to Twelve Month Business Plan

1. What is the main objective that I desire to achieve within the next six to twelve months?

2. What are the three main priorities I must accomplish for my goal to be achieved?

3. What are up to five strategies for each of the three priorities that can be measured and held accountable?

Step 7: Complete a Question Mind Exercise

1. What questions do I need to ask before worrying about having the answers?

2. What considerations do I need to question?

3. What are the key areas that need deeper questions?

4. What challenges or obstacles will I face?

5. What methods can I deploy to overcome or even prevent them?

6. Who can help me?

Step 8: Create an Opportunity Map (Organizational Chart)

1. What does the company look like in:
    a. One Year
    b. Three Years
    c. Five Years
    d. Someday

2. What key positions are required to support future growth?

3. Draw my organizational chart on paper.

Step 9: Identify Key Leadership Roles

1. What are the top five roles I will need to hire for?

2. What are the primary responsibilities for each of the five roles?

3. What performance metrics will they be held accountable to?

4. Describe the ideal person for each of the roles.

5. Build the bench, who do I currently know that could be a candidate?

Step 10: Build a Calendar of Training and Education

1. Personal Growth Calendar

   a. What does a personal growth calendar look like for me?

2. Customer Training & Education Calendar

   a. What does a training calendar look like for my customers?

3. Company Training & Education Calendar

   a. What does a training calendar look like for those I employ?

Step 11: Document Systems

1. What systems do I need to document and turn into a standard operating procedure manual?

2. What skills or methods do I take for granted that need to be documented?

3. What are the standards and expectations?

4. What are the key performance indicators that have the greatest impact on results?

Step 12: Develop a Marketing Strategy

1. Establish my brand.

   a. When people think of me, what do I want them to think of?

2. Establish my message.

   a. What voice, tonality, or message will speak directly to my target audience?

3. Establish my strategy.

   a. What methods am I going to use to reach them and where does my audience engage the most?

4. Establish my budget:

   a. Where are my marketing dollars best spent to achieve a return on investment (ROI)?

5. Establish my key performance indicators (KPIs).

   a. What are the key performance indicators I need to track to determine if my efforts are effective?

Step 13: Repurpose and Repackage

1. What can I currently repurpose to find ways to use the same thing in several different ways?

2. What can I currently repackage by taking something that may be old or stale and repackaging it so that it becomes interesting again?

The 13 Steps to Building a Scalable Business course provides a roadmap for you in any industry or business. It is not *the* way; it is just *a* way and is what worked for us when starting The Locker Room. Whether you utilize all the steps or just cherry-pick a few from the list, the choice is yours. This is the recipe and ingredients we used to build a successful business, and perhaps it will serve you too. Steps to success can appear boring and repetitive at times. Are you willing to accept the boredom associated with achieving a high level of mastery?

QUESTIONS TO CONSIDER:

1. What do I do exceptionally well that can be documented and systemized?

2. Which of the thirteen steps speaks to me the most? Why?

3. How has creativity worked against me?

4. What aspect of my business needs to focus on fundamentals?

5. Where am I being the most strategic in my business right now?

6. What area of my business or life do I need to intentionally slow down?

7. What is a company I admire that I can benchmark and research?

8. Who is a high achiever I admire that I can benchmark and research?

9. What skill am I currently discounting that others admire about me?

10. What topic could I teach to others because I feel that I have mastered it?

STOP AND COMPLETE:

In the spirit of mastering the fundamentals and following the breadcrumbs of high achievers, this exercise is focused on getting you in conversation with someone you consider a mentor or role model. The objective is to reach out to a mentor or role model, ask them for thirty minutes of their time, and interview them. I want you to direct your questions as specifically as you can regarding a challenge or opportunity you have in your business right now. Get very clear about what it is you want to learn from this individual so your questions are as clear, specific, and relevant as possible. If you cannot come up with anything specific right now, I have provided some questions for you in the Cannonball Workbook that work well when speaking with any mentor or role model.

CHAPTER 9

TOUCH THE LINE!

"The quality of a leader is reflected in the standards
they set for themselves."

RAY KROC

IF THIS, THEN THAT

Around the ages of eight and nine, our two daughters, while they are great kids in general, started really misbehaving towards one another. They would annoy each other and end up fighting more than ever before. My wife and I struggled to create boundaries until we relied on the trusted method of "if this, then that." For example, I remember taking them on a vacation, and we were going for a nice dinner at the resort that night. It had been one of those days where they were constantly fighting and we wanted to make sure we could start all over, course correct the behavior, and play offense rather than defense with their attitudes. My wife and I sat them down before dinner and said to them, "We are getting ready to go to a nice place for dinner. If you two cannot stop fighting, then we are going to leave, and you will lose out on all the swimming and fun we have planned for tomorrow. Do you understand?"

As simple as this may sound, children do not come with instruction manuals, and every personality and situation is different. What we quickly learned is that this method actually worked. Any time we would speak to them in advance about what was going to happen and the consequences of poor behavior, it set better behavior in motion. What I gathered from this is that standards and expectations matter. When we are willing to hold the line and communicate effectively, it serves as the carrot and the stick. We reward positive behavior and make clear that there is a consequence for poor behavior. I suppose that is parenting 101, right? Whatever we want to call it, the principle holds true. Setting standards upfront leads to success in any situation. Our ability to draw boundaries for ourselves allows us to communicate more effectively and stand firm for what we believe in to achieve our desired results.

A DIFFERENCE BETWEEN WINNING AND LOSING

I played college baseball from 2001 to 2006 for a team that was consistently ranked as one of the top five teams in the country. We had a Hall of Fame coach who was respected by every player who ever put on a uniform. Every year before the season, we would have to wake up at 4:30 a.m. to go lift weights at the campus gym. After we finished lifting, we would head out to the tennis courts to run what we called five by fives. The standard was that the team this year had to run twenty-five five by fives for each loss the team had during the previous year. So if we were entering the start of a new year and the prior season the team lost fifteen games, this year the team had to run twenty-five of them for each loss. That meant that for fifteen days after lifting, we would go to the tennis courts to check one off the list. What exactly is a five by five? On a tennis court, the players would line up on the line and have to sprint to the other end, touch the line, and repeat five different times. In other words, down back, down back, down equals a single five by five. We had to do twenty-five in a row to check one off for a loss the prior season. Running these drills was very simple. The two rules: you must sprint, and you must touch the line. If anyone was caught jogging or failed to touch the line, the standard was that the entire team would start over at zero.

I will never forget one of those mornings. All the players knew the standards and expectations, and the team was nearly finished with all twenty-five. In fact, we were at number twenty-four. As we were running, I remember the coach yelling, "STOP!" and every player came to immediate attention and froze. Our coach proceeded to tell us that someone did not touch the line, so the entire team had to start over at zero. As you may imagine, we were not happy. We were literally one away from being done and we had to start all over. Consider the alternative for a moment. What if our coach saw the player stop a few inches short of the line and let it go? What if our coach decided to turn his head in the opposite direction and pretend he never saw it happen? He easily could have done that, but he didn't. Why? Because the standards and expectations were clear. He was willing to take a stand for our greatness even when he knew how much it would upset the team. He did not let us slack for a single moment. The standard was very simple; you must touch the line. If you do not touch the line, then the consequence is to start over.

Nothing about that was unclear. Because it is a team sport, the entire team had to begin at zero because the actions of one impacted the whole team.

Although I was not happy at the moment nor questioned what lesson I could learn from it, I never forgot that morning and have learned to appreciate what happened that day. I understand now that our coach was preparing us to become men of integrity. He knew exactly what he was doing and how important it was. We may not have liked it or understood it at the moment, but he knew that later in life, we would eventually get it. What he showed us that morning was that standards matter, and there are consequences for breaching those standards. I am incredibly grateful for the tough love he exhibited by upholding the standard—touch the line.

LESSONS AND SUCCESS PRINCIPLES
You Don't Necessarily Push People, You Hold Standards

Transparent communication is one of the core values of our business. One of the reasons it is a core value is because it allows for proactive and transparent communication to avoid misunderstandings. Our core values represent the standards and principles by which we operate. In business, people do not necessarily do business with us as an individual. They do business with us because of the standards we represent. We could be highly likable people, but if our standards are low, they will likely take their business elsewhere. Conversely, if we have a product or service in a saturated space, we may earn business with a similar product or service, but we represent a higher set of standards. To hold standards, I have followed a four-step process that has served us well. The four steps include:

1. Establish your standards.

2. Communicate your standards.

3. Constantly remind others of your standards.

4. Live out loud with your actions.

Knowing it begins with establishing our standards, the next logical question we should ask is, "What are my standards?" To help with this, it requires our willingness to go internal and explore what we value the most. It also requires us to categorize the standards we are creating. Are we creating performance standards for others? Are we creating cultural standards for the organization? Are we creating standards for client care? For any function of a business, it should have standardized processes along with standards that create a boundary around the core functions. Similarly, we must establish standards for ourselves and how we engage with others. What are the non-negotiables in our life? How will we know when someone crosses a line?

Two quotes speak to me the most when I discuss establishing standards for business or personal. The first is, "You teach people how to treat you." The second is, "You cannot complain about the things you tolerate." Actions speak louder than words, and our actions are also the professor who teaches others how they should interact with us. When we allow someone to take advantage of us or speak to us in a condescending tone then we are endorsing that behavior. However, when we are clear about our values and standards, we can plant our feet firmly in the ground and let the other person know that their behavior is unacceptable. This does not mean it has to be confrontational. In fact, I would argue it should be "care-frontational." It is because we care about our relationship with the other person that we are willing to speak up and let them know we are not feeling appreciated in that moment. I am not advocating that we seek arguments or suggesting that everyone adapt to our way. Relationships are a two-way street built on mutual respect. Success is found when both parties acknowledge the standards of one another and respect them. I remember my college baseball coach always saying, "You do not have to agree with me, but you do need to respect me." In the context of performance standards, we should consider these key areas: specific, achievable, easy to understand, relevant to the position, and easy to measure. Sounds familiar to S.M.A.R.T. goals, doesn't it?

There is a wonderful example that has circulated on social media over the years. The story is about a baseball coach, John Scolinos, speaking on stage at a major baseball convention. During his animated and passionate speech, Scolinos pointed out that a home plate in baseball is seventeen inches wide. Pitchers are held to a standard to throw a baseball over the seventeen-inch home plate, which would determine if it was a ball or a strike. The outcome is very clear because a pitcher either threw the ball across the plate or he did not. If he threw the ball over home plate, then it was a strike; if he did not, it was a ball. The rules of the game are simple. In his story, Scolinos argued that widening the plate would change the rules of the game and diminish the teams having a fair shot at winning according to the written rules. He used this example as a lesson to all coaches and parents in attendance at the convention by linking it to how we raise our children along with how we carry ourselves. He challenged the room during his speech to consider what standards each person accepts in their lives. Are we widening the plate to make the game easier? Are we bending the rules a little bit? Or are we keeping the standard and demanding to operate with integrity according to the rules of the game? It is a great lesson, and I highly encourage everyone to read the full article, which can be found in Chris Sperry's "Baseball Thoughts" column at www.sperrybaseballlife.com.

Communicating Standards

Once our personal and professional standards are documented, we are ready to move on to the second step, communicating our standards. This is commonly referred to as setting proper expectations. I have found that this step works best when we are proactive instead of reactive. For example, whenever I have hired a new coach for our organization, we go through a series of meetings to determine if we are aligned. One of the stages before presenting an offer to partner together is called the expectations dialogue. I will begin the conversation by reviewing our company's mission, core values, and belief system. From there, I will review the standards document that shows the standards we hold our coaches accountable to, and I will ask the person to initial next to each standard, acknowledging they have read, understood, and agreed to the standard before we move any further. Of course, this generally opens up dialogue and questions so both sides are crystal clear on the standards to perform at a high level within the organization. For further clarification that outlines the entire process, I have provided the template we use below when hiring someone:

Items Needed for Meeting:

1. Company mission, core values, belief system, and goals

2. Job description for the role

3. 90-day goals, expectations, and performance metrics

4. 90-day training and development plan

5. First 90-day expectations dialogue worksheet

Order of Operations for the Meeting:

1. Review company's mission, core values, and belief system along with company goals

2. Review job description and how role fits into the company's vision

3. Review 90-day goals, expectations, and performance metrics

4. Review 90-day training and development plan

5. Set expectation for the 90-day evaluation dialogue

6. Ask for any questions or concerns before moving forward

The First 90 Days Expectations Dialogue worksheet is intended to serve as a guide and flow for the conversation so the meeting can be effective and efficient. A PDF of this worksheet is available at www.jake-dixon.com. You can make notes as you go, so there is a recording of the commitments and conversations that took place. A best practice would be to keep a copy in the candidate's file for future reference, if necessary.

This worksheet provides for great conversations that hit on the critical components prior to going into business with one another. Failure to have this conversation can lead to resentment. Resentment can live in the gaps between expectations and reality. Think back to a time when you were disappointed by someone else. You entered the situation with expectations of what would happen, how they would behave, and what the outcome would be. Contrary to your expectations, things did not go according to how you envisioned it. You became frustrated and built resentment toward the other person, which caused friction and damage to the relationship. It fractured the trust and made you second guess whether you were interested in further pursuing things. What created this resentment in the first place? How could this have been avoided? Expectations can be a tricky thing because we operate with them but rarely communicate them to the other party involved. In this example, when it looked like an agreement was going to be made, pausing to communicate your expectations could have prevented disappointment and misunderstanding. It would have also given the other individual an opportunity to share what their expectations were as well so everyone would be on the same page.

When teaching other business coaches to set proper expectations with clients, I will commonly use the example I personally utilized when beginning a new coaching relationship with someone. I would challenge them to answer these questions:

- What are my expectations of the client?
- What can they expect of me?
- How will performance and standards be measured?

I would emphasize to the coach how critical it is to be firm and upfront about the expectations. The following exemplifies what we feel is essential during early dialogues with a new coaching client. For example:

> *"I am so excited to work with you (Name)! Now that we have spent time getting to know each other and understanding how we can guarantee a 10+ experience for you, I'd like to set proper expectations regarding our*

time together, especially with one-on-one coaching sessions. Is that fair? Great! From my experience, during our time together over the next year, you will likely have three to five incredibly powerful one-on-one sessions with me. You may be surprised by this since we will have far more than just three to five interactions with each other. Those three to five life-changing sessions will lead to massive transformation if you are willing to embrace them, follow through, and do the work. On the other hand, most of our time together will be more about maintenance. May I explain?

It is just like your car; typically, it is the maintenance checks performed on your car that are most critical because they ensure the car is running with optimal performance. The oil changes, tire rotation, and basic diagnostic checks, when the check engine light comes on, are often the most important to guarantee your vehicle will run smoothly and in good health. Your business is no different. The way I see it, I am the mechanic for your business. Every time we meet, I will assume your check engine light is on. My job is to press the reset button once we determine that things are operating in a healthy manner. This will ensure your business vehicle is functioning with optimal performance. So again, most of our time together will be conducting maintenance checks and then a handful will likely be life-changing and lead to significant change. Does that make sense?"

I would explain to the coach that after this dialogue, they will be able to remind the client if "value" ever comes into question. We took the stance that it is the client's responsibility to show up for sessions with a plan of action in mind, challenges to discuss, and determine the one thing they want to get out of the session with us. We did everything to avoid them expecting us to come up with the topic every time because they just wanted someone to tell them what to do. We refused to allow them to walk into our office like a bowling ball and expect us to throw them down the lane so they could knock down all the pins. Our philosophy is to be the bumpers on the side of the gutters and simply keep them on track toward their goals.

Constantly Remind Others of Our Standards

After establishing our standards and effectively communicating them, we must constantly remind others about them. This cannot be a conversation that occurs one time and is never revisited again. Numerous occasions in business have required me to sit down with someone and revisit what we had both answered and agreed to during the setting of expectations dialogue. By doing so, it took emotion out of the equation, and we were able to reflect on our own words and recenter ourselves. This level of open communication and respect is not possible if we do not have the conversation and document things every step of the way. I have worked with hundreds of leaders in the real estate industry, and an example of this is when I crafted an article titled "16 Things Every Great Leader Must Know." The reason I drafted this article was because of my experience and witnessing firsthand the constant struggles and frustrations leaders would go through. To create a reference point and continually remind themselves of standards and expectations in a very challenging business, I wrote the following:

1. We cannot want it more for someone than they want it for themselves. This is the single greatest lesson I had to learn as a leader, and it is a difficult one. As they say, we cannot push a rope. With the low barrier of entry into the business and the high percentage that are no longer in the business within two years—we can only do so much as leaders. What makes it difficult is that we often see the best in someone else. We see their God-given talents and unique qualities that make them who they are. Our role is to extract their talents and highlight them as the center of their success, so they operate within their strength zone. Time is always the great equalizer, and it is fascinating how some agents' businesses skyrocket their first year, and others do not. We all know their achievements boil down to their commitment to attaining their goals and having the motivation from within. It can be frustrating as a leader to see so much potential in an agent who is not fulfilling their potential, making it very hard for us to ever give up on them. We must remember that we can throw out the life jacket if someone is drowning; however, it is their job to grab on and allow you to pull them safely to shore. Meeting people where they are is a hard lesson to learn, and yet, as long as we can look in the mirror and say we have done everything to encourage, inspire, engage, and pour ourselves into that agent, then we can be at peace about the efforts and attitude we have control over.

2. We must have careful and candid conversations. This can be a struggle for some because we have a complex of being confrontational. For me, it required a very intentional focus to grow in this area because I wanted to be liked by everyone. The reality is that it is not a popularity contest, and we must get out of our own way and do what is right for our agents. We must operate from a foundational belief that people don't care how much we know until they know how much we care. We earn the right to have candid conversations. It is possible that we love someone so much that we love them right out of the business. If we are not willing to say what needs to be said in the best interest of the agent, then we need to evaluate this area. Undoubtedly, all leaders have a heart for serving others, which is why we must be able to have real conversations and say the things that need to be said or ask questions that no one else is willing to ask. Oddly enough, when we survey the agents, the primary expectation they have in a strong leader is the capability to hold them accountable and willing to take a stand for their greatness more than they are willing to take a stand for their own limiting beliefs.

3. We do not have to know it all. Leaders often feel like they must be "the" answer; the end all be all expert to everything that may arise. Authenticity is one of the greatest gifts a leader could give their team, which comes with the willingness to accept that they do not know everything. Our ability to stay vulnerable and admit when we do not have all the answers makes us relatable. Our job as leaders is not necessarily to provide all the answers, but rather to facilitate an environment conducive to their success. When we encourage others to be resourceful and not necessarily see us as the resource, we create a group of people who are not completely dependent on us. Instead, we create agents who are independent business owners. It is a slippery slope if the leader becomes the product. Many leaders understand that their job is not to be the reason why someone should be successful, but rather simply serve as messengers to deliver the models and systems that they know work while holding people in alignment, so they achieve their goals.

4. Be the chief accountability officer and drive five core items. A leader's value lies in holding the team accountable for the goals *they* set for themselves. This is achieved by constantly speaking the language of business through numbers. Numbers take the emotion out of any conversation so we can see things for what they are. Serving as their chief accountability officer is a primary responsibility to help others get what *they* said they wanted from this career. The five core items we drive to do this are mindset, activities, results, skillset development, and systems. Everything begins with having the proper mindset. When confident, they will take accountable actions that align with their strengths. Thus, holding them accountable for the proper actions, behaviors, and habits becomes the next element in the sequence. Are they caught up in the busyness of the job or are they being productive? The third core item is results. We can have as much fun as we want leading others on the first two; however, if it does not lead to the desired results, then are we being effective? Business is supposed to fund their perfect life, which cannot be achieved without tangible results. Skillset development is the fourth core item a leader is responsible for helping their team with. We must constantly help them reflect and sharpen the sword of how they can be better. A skill can always be developed or refined which puts them on a constant pursuit towards success. Lastly, are systems and processes. Our job is not to preach "more, more, more," leading to burnout. We must help them develop systems and processes so they can achieve results in an efficient and predictable manner. If a leader can master driving these five core items and not get hung up on distractions, they will be an extremely effective and well-respected leader.

5. Track numbers. People grow into the conversations we create around them. Numbers are the language of business, and most people will do everything in their power to avoid numbers. It is our responsibility as leaders to help them know their numbers and treat their business like it is a business. If they are not running their business by numbers, that means they are running it out of emotion and unsure how that will turn out. Our job as leaders is to create amazing small business owners. Are we treating our agents like CEOs or just teaching them how to create a contract? The destination is not to get them to their goal; it is to help them flourish and have an amazing business that funds their life. By teaching them to understand core metrics such as: conversion rates and leading indicators that lead to the lagging indicators, we are preparing them with a skillset of how to run a business effectively. We can help them build awareness and serve as the doctors of their real estate business. How can we diagnose the issue or prescribe the right medication if we are unaware of the vital signs or health of our agent's business?

6. Ask powerful questions vs. telling them what to do. Asking powerful questions is an art form that takes practice. It is very tempting for a leader to feel the need to have all the answers, and, therefore, tell others what to do rather than helping them discover the answer on their own. Keep in mind that what worked for us may not work for everyone. It is important to remove our personal opinions and biases from many of the interactions. Instead, come from curiosity and ask questions that lead the person to their own discovery. When they are the author of the commitment and strategy, then they are the owners of the outcome. If we are telling them what they should do, then they may not have complete buy in or may end up faulting us for lack of results. There are moments when we must call the plays from the sidelines, but it does not mean they can't call an audible and change the play before snapping the ball. Lead a team of quarterbacks who can adjust accordingly based on the flow of the game. Remember, the coaches are standing on the sidelines, and it is the players who are playing the game. Games are won during practice, so how are we preparing our players during this time? Are they creating their own strategies and playbook based on their personal goals, strengths, and behavior styles? This will help us remain a third party who asks powerful questions rather than telling them what they should do.

7. Know the difference between coaching and training in business. Coaching is all about development. It is unlocking someone's potential to maximize their performance. It is helping them learn rather than teaching (or training) them. The underlying intent of every coaching interaction is to build awareness, responsibility, and self-belief in the mind of the agent. We know that true leadership teaches people how to think so they can get what they want, when they want it. A leader has the uncanny ability to light the fire from within someone instead of a trainer who may light the fire underneath someone. Here are some key distinctions to consider: 1) Coaching enhances knowledge, and training transfers knowledge. 2) Coaching focuses on what to do with a skill, and training focuses on how to do a skill. 3) Coaching is usually one-on-one, whereas training is often in a group setting. 4) Coaching is usually conversational, whereas training is usually unilateral. 5) Coaching is development-focused, and training is learning-focused. 6) Coaching depends on asking, whereas training depends on telling. 7) Coaching facilitates central thinking and decision-making, whereas training usually has no follow-up accountability. Coaching uses a "care-frontational" approach, which may mean uncomfortable conversations about bad habits, limiting beliefs, or anything else that may hinder their success.

8. We cannot motivate; we can only inspire. A common question leaders ask is, "How do I motivate my agents so they stay engaged?" The hard truth is, unfortunately, we cannot motivate them. We can only inspire them. When we initially meet with an agent, we must dig deep into their goals, dreams, and current realities. It is through this process that we learn what their "Big Why" is and what pain results in not achieving that. Through coaching, we can ask powerful questions to re-align that person with their Big Why. This results in motivation for the individual that comes from within them, which translates into action. When we can understand the pain versus pleasure conversation, then we can inspire anyone to get into action. Logic makes people think, and emotion makes people act. Use this principle by getting others emotional about their goals. Rarely do leaders discuss the negative pain points with someone, yet we know people are typically moving away from pain as motivation rather than moving towards pleasure. If we are only coaching and leading to the pleasure aspect, then it is not enough. We must incorporate the pain associated with lack of achievement because this is a fundamental truth that will motivate someone to move in the right direction.

9. Have a coach or mentor. How can we ask our agents to engage in our leadership if we are not investing to grow our own? Every leader must have a coach or mentor to grow and remain accountable to. Leaders must model the behavior they expect of their team. When the leader has a coach or mentor, it shows that they are learning and growing. It demonstrates a willingness to be vulnerable and be held accountable by someone else. It illustrates to others that we are in the trenches with them and brings authenticity to the conversation when we share what our coach or mentor is having us work on.

10. Use proven leadership models. Follow the breadcrumbs and stop winging it. Many great leaders use models in their approach to coaching and leading others. It is important to work on mastering our leadership to have effective conversations. Leaders have a huge responsibility to serve others, and if we are only leaning on our past experiences to guide them, we are missing a huge element. Our experience and raw knowledge won't serve them to the capacity they deserve. Following proven leadership models allows us to dig deeper and follow a roadmap. It allows us to be more intentional as a leader, so we can guide the conversation to the outcome necessary to advance the person's business. What models are we leveraging to be a more effective leader?

11. Show recognition and appreciation. Some people claim they do not need the recognition moments, but who are we kidding? Everyone appreciates the recognition and the feeling of being appreciated. As they say about recognition, babies cry for it, and grown men and women die for it. When leading others, we must develop our own system of appreciation and recognition strategies. It is not uncommon for someone to work harder to see their name on a wall or a trophy than they will for a commission check. A culture of productivity needs to appeal to all behavioral styles. If we are an I or D personality in the D.I.S.C. profile, then we may want recognition for a job well done through results. If we are an S or C personality, then we may desire a job well done to gain assurance that we are doing the right things and to stay the course. No matter the behavioral style, how will we honor those in our world who deserve it? For a long time, I heard agents mumble about team meetings and how the top agents always got the recognition. We began doing a variety of things to honor the agents who had a great week with activities or maybe have just shown tenacity and commitment with no result so far. Mix it up and have fun with this!

12. It is just as much about life coaching as it is about business. There are many different styles and approaches to leading others. Based on my experience, leadership can be disguised as life coaching. Typically, we can take a scenario someone is going through and identify the greater principle to which it applies. For example, imagine an agent who is consistently not meeting their goals or showing up late to appointments. A question I may ask is, "Where else might this be showing up in your life?" How they participate here is how they are likely participating everywhere, so we can relate it to other areas within their life to speak through analogies. It can be easy to get caught up in lead generation or time blocking, so we must keep the human element to what we do and relate things back to life principles. Transformation is an inside-out project. Everyone has goals and desires to lead an amazing life or achieve a certain level of income, yet are they willing to do the things someone else has done to achieve that level of success? It goes back to personal growth. Whom must they become first? Then, what does a person of that success level do to have the things that they have? We can't miss opportunities to listen to what our team is saying, as well as what they are not saying, during our time together. Examine the life lessons that can be pulled from a business experience and coach them on it. This is just as much of a personal growth quest for many as it is being successful in business.

13. Create a culture of productivity. Everyone likes to be a part of something bigger than themselves. When someone explores joining our business, it is vitally important that we share our vision and goals with them. It allows them the opportunity to feel a sense of community, belonging, and significance to a greater mission. As leaders, we must realize we are responsible for creating a magnetic culture that others are attracted to. Our culture should demonstrate a shared vision, purpose, and goal while creating a sense of community. Inherently, it creates a culture and level of accountability where the team is pushing one another, and they are willing to share successes and failures with one another for the overall good of the team. Together, everyone achieves more.

14. Engagement will be our biggest struggle. It goes without saying that getting team engagement relates to an earlier point about not being able to want it more for someone else than they want it for themselves. Data proves engaged agents earn more income than those who drift into isolation. Thankfully, there are systems we can implement as leaders to enhance engagement across the company.

It all starts with expectations. We must constantly communicate the importance to agents about staying engaged, tracking numbers, showing up to training events, and scheduling their appointments with us. I often say that the two evils in life are boredom and isolation. Boredom should be impossible if someone is engaging since real estate is a relationship business, and we are talking to people every day. Thus, I do not worry about the boredom factor if they are showing up and doing the right activities. However, I worry most about isolation. It is the greatest downfall, and it comes in a couple of different forms. Many agents slowly drift away from the pack and become lone wolves because they realize this business is not as easy as they thought, and it requires a lot of hard work. They often quit before they even get started, and they stop showing up to meetings and appointments and stop engaging in the office due to entering with incorrect expectations. Another reason they drift into isolation is because they fall victim to their own success. Suddenly, they experience success, so they think they are an expert. Therefore, they stop plugging into training because they get complacent or feel they know it all since they have already attended a class. The reality is, that unless they can teach the material for others to understand, they have not mastered anything. As leaders, we must watch out for signs of disengagement and be proactive in reaching out to get them plugged back into the culture.

15. Take a stance for their greatness. The four most powerful words someone may need to hear is, "I believe in you." This goes back to asking ourselves: "Am I willing to stand up for their greatness more than they are willing to stand up for their own limiting beliefs?" I remind my team frequently that it is not a popularity contest for me, and there will be days they do not like me, which is okay. As a mentor of mine would say, "I care more about them than I care about our relationship." Think about that for a second. We must be willing to say what needs to be said to protect the best interests of the team members, even if that means being unpopular or feeling like we are standing alone on an island. We must follow our instincts and allow people to judge us based on our intentions, not necessarily the outcomes. Our team should never question our intentions, knowing they come from the heart. Every leader has a different personality type, so however it manifests for us, it is important that our team knows we are their number one fan and advocate. Stand by them through the hard times and the good times and watch how loyalty and trust become contagious. If our team ever needs to borrow some belief in themselves, they should first turn to us, and we can lend them some.

16. Follow proven systems. We may have no need to reinvent the wheel or get creative. Sometimes, leaders are simply the advocates and messengers for what already exists. A good leader sounds like a broken record on purpose. Agents will get exhausted hearing us say the same things repeatedly, yet we know what works and what will always work. Stay the course. Continue to rely on the systems and models provided that are proven to work. It is okay to repackage the same thing in a different way so it becomes interesting to our team again, i.e., lead generation. Simultaneously, success can be boring, repetitious, and mundane. Organizations need to accept the boredom associated with mastery. As we have said, most agents just need the basic principles of the business without any fancy sauce put on it. The blocking and tackling of this game are fundamental. Real estate is a contact sport; our agents just need to get their jerseys dirty. I hope reading through this example provides some insights. Creating a reference point for standards and expectations is critical, especially when we can have frequent discussions to keep everyone aligned.

Documentation will always beat conversation; however, when the two are combined, it creates a powerful recipe for success.

Be Consistent and Live Out Loud

The final element is to live out loud and remain consistent. In our organization, every month, we have a video conference with our entire team of coaches and staff. The first fifteen minutes of each meeting are dedicated to our "Culture in Action." This is where we pour into each other by referencing items from our core values and beliefs as a company that is well documented and show appreciation for someone on the team living these ideals out loud. By doing this each month, it allows us to keep focus and never forget who we are. It holds us accountable to the core values and beliefs we all agreed to as part of the standard to be with our company. The energy is contagious and sets the tone for the entire meeting. It is one thing to establish standards, document those standards, and consistently communicate our expectations; however, it takes an entirely new meaning when we deploy a system that requires us to consistently live those standards out loud and demonstrate them to the world. A movement is created when a group of individuals share a common set of values and beliefs and work unapologetically daily toward a mission to demonstrate them. For any business I have ever run, this formula has created a magnetic culture that fosters success for everyone.

QUESTIONS TO CONSIDER:

1. What standards do I expect of myself?
2. What are my non-negotiables?

3. How do I effectively communicate my standards and expectations to others?

4. When was a time that I felt disappointed because standards and expectations were not addressed upfront?

5. What new boundaries do I need to create for myself?

6. What actions am I taking that are currently incongruent with my own standards?

7. What number stood out the most from the 16 Things? Why?

8. How can I see myself using the expectations dialogue in the future?

9. What is the takeaway from the "Don't Widen the Plate" story?

10. What is my commitment to standards, moving forward?

STOP AND COMPLETE:

To assist with establishing your standards, it helps to first establish your core values. In other words, your standards are a byproduct of gaining clarity around your core values. The exercise is from a class I wrote called "Success Through Others: How to Find, Attract, Hire, and Retain Talent" and can be found in your Cannonball Workbook.

CHAPTER 10

SOMETIMES YOU JUST HAVE TO LAUGH

"Humility is not thinking less of yourself,
it's thinking of yourself less."

C.S. LEWIS

DUCT TAPE FIXES EVERYTHING

When our daughters were seven and eight, we took them on a one-week Royal Caribbean cruise for our family vacation. We were joined by my parents, sister, and brother-in-law. We went all-in for this trip by getting a large suite at the back of the ship and had planned our excursions well in advance for every port of call. The excursion our daughters looked forward to the most was swimming with the dolphins. It was a dream of theirs and finally was about to come true. The evening before swimming with the dolphins, our oldest daughter was so excited that she could hardly contain herself. She was running around the room, and right next to the end of the bed was the bathroom. The bathroom door was open and when she went to jump onto the bed, she somehow caught the back of her foot perfectly on the edge of the door. She screamed in pain and was afraid to look down to see how bad it was. My wife and I both rushed to see what was wrong and saw a deep gash on the back of her foot. We instantly looked at each other, not saying a word, but the expression said it all. It was bad, and we both knew it. This was not just a scratch; it was a very deep cut that needed immediate attention.

How could this happen the night before the big dolphin adventure? Moments before, she was the happiest girl in the world, and now she was crying in pain with a serious injury. We scrambled to the phone, and luckily, the ship had a doctor on board. They were getting ready to close for the evening, but we were fortunate enough for them to take our daughter down to receive medical attention. A while later, she returned to the room with several stitches to help heal the wound. Thankfully, she would be okay, but what about the dolphins? How could she fulfill her dreams of swimming with dolphins the next day when she had a huge cut on her foot? We were convinced she would have to sit it out because everything said not to put a fresh cut like that in salt water. It was a crushing blow to us as a family and more so for our oldest daughter.

We were not willing to stop there. We wanted to explore all ways to still make this possible for her because we felt so bad. We made a post in a social media group specific to this particular cruise, asking if anyone had waterproof bandages. Finally, a kind lady responded, saying she had bandages, but none were waterproof. At this point, we would take anything. Furthermore, I dialed the maintenance team to ask if they could bring us duct tape. Yes, duct tape. I thought, if we could put a bandage on, wrap her foot in a plastic bag, and then secure it tightly with duct tape, maybe it would become waterproof long enough to allow her to do the dolphin adventure. It was a crazy idea, but desperate times called for desperate measures.

The next day came around, and we were determined to at least try it. So my wife and I executed the plan and created a homemade covering out of bandages, plastic bags, and a lot of duct tape. We set out to get off the ship that morning and even had our daughter in a wheelchair since it was so difficult for her to walk. We could not help but laugh at how ridiculous this idea even was. Here we had our oldest daughter limping around, then riding in a wheelchair, with duct tape wrapped around her leg for all to see. We had no shame because we would never see these people again, and after all, dolphins were more important. When we arrived at the excursion, it was the moment of truth. She proceeded to limp down the dock and reluctantly get into the water for the excursion to begin. We had the most amazing time and plenty of pictures to prove it. When we got out of the water, we raced to peek under the duct tape, and sure enough, it was perfectly dry. We could not believe it actually worked! We laughed hysterically that it worked. Sometimes, life delivers us a curveball. As ridiculous as something may seem, success requires ingenuity and humility. The road is going to be difficult, but if we can learn to laugh at ourselves, we can turn upsetting big things into small things. To this day, we still laugh about how ridiculous our plan was and how it worked. The principle has left a lasting impact on all of us. Do not be afraid to laugh and have fun along the way. Whether success is defined as riding a dolphin for the first time or achieving the wealth you desire, do not take yourself too seriously along the way, and remember to have fun.

YOU WANT ME TO DO WHAT?

As you know by now, I played college baseball in Florida from 2001 to 2006. I owe so much of my success and who I am today to what I have learned over the years. When I accepted a full-ride scholarship to play, I never knew exactly what I was getting myself into. I knew it was a highly successful program with a Hall of Fame coach and that it would be tough. What I did not fully comprehend was something the players had to do every year called "The Flex Off." The Flex Off occurred every year on campus just before we left for winter break in December. The moment we stepped foot on campus in August, we had to lift weights every morning at 4:30 a.m. and then go to class until 1:00 p.m. to be on the field for afternoon practice. Lifting weights was not only for strength and conditioning, but it was also motivating, knowing we had The Flex Off in a few months.

The Flex Off was where we were broken down into different weight classes and then went on stage in front of hundreds of sorority women to do a flexing routine as if we were bodybuilders. Right before the next weight class took the stage, we would all go into the restroom and lather up in baby oil, so we glistened under the bright lights. Many players would go to tanning beds in the weeks ahead to prepare for this night. As a young man who was six feet six inches tall and one hundred ninety pounds soaking wet, I can assure you I was not exactly considered a specimen for others to look at. Being from a town of seven hundred people in the sticks of Illinois never prepared me for a moment like this. Although it never happened to me, many of my teammates were so nervous before going out that they would physically get sick in the restroom as we were getting ready.

Needless to say, I did not exactly look forward to The Flex Off every year. While some players deserved to show off their muscles on stage,

I was not one of them. I was good at playing the game, but I was not the epitome of a bodybuilder. I distinctly remember our coach telling us players, "If you can do this, you can do anything. You can make a presentation in front of a board of directors or deliver a keynote speech in front of thousands." I did not appreciate his words at the time, but looking back, I understand. He was preparing us for success. If we had the courage to stand on stage flexing our muscles in front of hundreds of women each year, then was it so difficult to make a sales pitch to a small group of investors? I appreciate the lessons he instilled in us during those years. I now recognize the importance of humility and being able to laugh at myself. I learned that I loved playing the game so much that I was willing to go through things I did not necessarily enjoy. I was willing to do what it took to earn playing time so I could stand on the pitcher's mound with a ball in my hand, ready to compete. One way to look at it is that your ability to succeed may depend on your willingness to be embarrassed, show humility, and even fail.

LESSONS AND SUCCESS PRINCIPLES
Funny Equals Money

I remember the first time my mentor said, "Funny = Money" during a training I attended in 2011. As simple as it sounds, I never embraced that until I heard him say it. I felt as if I had to uphold some image others expected me to be or that I could never be my authentic self. Behind the scenes, I love to crack jokes and make others laugh but something in me felt I had to be polished and always professional in the working world. When I embraced the fact that funny equals money, everything changed. I was able to step into my normal behavioral style, and I credit this single concept to growing multiple businesses ever since. My kids may argue that I am not that funny, and I am certainly no stand-up comedian; however, when I am able to freely express myself without worrying about the judgment of others, it is incredibly empowering. I bet the same is true for you too.

The advice of "fake it until you make it" is a joke in and of itself. The idea that we should pretend we are someone that we are not violates all success principles. I will never forget building a large organization for the largest direct sales company in the world that happened to be in the health and fitness space. I fully embraced the funny equals money concept. I thought back to high school when I was voted the one with "Most School Spirit" in my senior year for the yearbook. Anything I would do, I always let humor and laughter lead the way. I would play all-in and dress in the most ridiculous outfits during homecoming week. I just loved making other people laugh, even if it was at my own expense.

I applied this same enthusiasm when building my direct sales business. In fact, a highlight moment occurred in 2010, when I attended my first large event with the company. Tens of thousands of direct sales professionals were present, and one of my best friends and I decided to get green body suits that covered us from head to toe. We could see through the body suit but from the outside looking in, it was just two large men in green tights. During an afterparty event, the music was playing, and everyone was dancing. The founders and other leaders were on stage leading the way, and my friend and I worked our way up to the front of the stage. The founder of the company spotted us and called us up onto the stage. There we were in all our glory, dancing away in front of thousands of people in our green body suits. It turned out this was legendary for our businesses because, as soon as the green men were revealed, people wanted to take their pictures with us. We went viral on social media for how ridiculous we looked.

From that moment forward, it showed others we had humility. We could laugh at ourselves and have fun while building a business. We both rose to the top one percent of income earners inside of the company, and I credit a large reason for that being our willingness to be funny and not take ourselves so seriously.

What prevents most people from playing all-in and expressing themselves in a genuine way? For me, it brings up a model I learned a while ago, which is the four stages of competence. The four stages of competence are as follows:

- **Unconscious incompetence (ignorance)**—This is someone who does not understand or know how to do something and does not even know there is a gap. This is where people will say, "I don't know what I don't know." Initially, they may deny the usefulness of the skill or behavior. The individual must recognize their own incompetence and the value of the new skill or behavior, before moving on to the next stage.

- **Conscious incompetence (awareness)**—In this case, someone does not know how to do something, but they do recognize the gap or blind spot along with the value of a new skill or behavior. Many times, this is where experimentation happens and failing forward toward success applies.

- **Conscious competence (learning)**—Here, someone knows how to do something. However, doing the skill or new behavior requires concentration. This is generally where a system or process applies because it breaks things down into repeatable steps. Think back to baking a cake and following the instructions on the back of the box. Unless we can do it without thinking, it is an example of conscious competence.

- **Unconscious competence (mastery)**—Someone who has had a significant amount of time on task over time that it has become "second nature." It is essentially involuntary, where we do not have to think; we just react and do. As a result, the skill or behavior can be performed while executing another task. The person may be knowledgeable enough to teach it to others. An example is just like driving a car to work. We do not have to think about it; we just automatically know what to do.[11]

The reason this model comes to mind is because, until something like "funny equals money" is brought to our awareness, we may be completely oblivious to the fact that it even exists. However, once we gain awareness, then we can begin applying a new behavior. We can experiment, refine, and ultimately master a new skill or behavior. Remember, we can't take ourselves so seriously that we forget to have fun along the way. We can let our personality shine through our work. Having this level of humility will lead us to more sustainable and fulfilling success in the future.

We Are Perfectly Imperfect

"Perfection is overrated, boring. It's the imperfections--the vulnerabilities, the weaknesses, the human elements--that make us who we are, that make us real, beautiful . . . necessary."

GUY HARRISON

When it comes to humility and achieving our definition of success, it is important to note one of my guiding beliefs in everything I do. Harry Truman said, "Imperfect action is better than perfect inaction." Leading up to that, I had been so concerned about my image and making mistakes. I would fear what others might say or think of me. I felt I was demonstrating weakness when I wanted others to see me as strong and competent. It forced me to put my ego aside and stop worrying about being right or concerning myself with what others thought. I decided to take a stand for myself and show up with complete humility. It took me stepping out in faith, saying that I do not know everything, and I am going to make a lot of mistakes. Doing this led me to take bigger and bolder actions because I stopped caring about everyone else and put my dreams front and center. Admitting I make mistakes was extremely liberating. However, although I acknowledged my mistakes and imperfections, I would always make a point to back that up by letting others know I would not let them down. They see that I am a leader who has humility because of my willingness to fail forward. I will dust myself off and stand back up when I take a hit. It demonstrates that I am completely okay with being flawed rather than trying to put on a flawless front.

I wrote a course called "The Champion's Mindset," where I discussed how people may refer to us as fearless leaders. I make the argument that I do not want to be referred to as fearless. Perhaps I am playing semantics, but I never want to set the expectation that I think I am perfect, or that I am not afraid, or that I do not experience imposter syndrome from time to time as well. I am very much a fearful leader; it is just that I can quickly convert my fear into fuel. I do not let it hold me back; I leverage it to propel me forward. Where are we holding ourselves back right now because we are too worried about being perfect? What action are we not taking out of fear that we might mess up? What have we tried once and failed at that we need to return and try again? Imperfect action beats perfect inaction. Would we rather take decisive action to advance boldly in the direction of our dreams, or would we rather retreat fearfully into a world of mediocrity? People make mistakes, so what? John Maxwell titled a popular book of his *Sometimes You Win Sometimes You Learn*.[12] Legendary coach John Wooden said, "If you're not making mistakes, then you're not doing anything. I'm positive that a doer makes mistakes."

To accept mistakes and vulnerability with our actions, requires us to have humility. We are not going to be perfect, and we are not going to know everything. And that is okay! When we stay true to ourselves and stop looking to others for acceptance, that is where we find true joy and happiness—two words we would likely use to describe success. Instead of looking for external approval, we must get clear on looking internally first. Where do we turn to find inspiration and positive energy? Here are some categories to explore:

Physical: This includes how you take care of your body through health, nutrition, and physical fitness.

Spiritual: This includes connecting with your higher power; an energy source greater than your own.

Relational: This includes deep connection, love, and personal relationships to keep you centered.

Financial: This includes your wealth, work, and financial well-being.

Mental: This includes your personal growth and development to keep a healthy mindset.

Perfection is overrated and unattainable. Remember when we discussed S.M.A.R.T. goals earlier, and one of the core elements was "A" for attainable? It is easy to place unrealistic expectations on ourselves because we are trying to pursue something that does not exist. Rather than pursuing perfection, pursue excellence. Aristotle is credited for saying, "We are what we repeatedly do. Excellence, therefore, is not an act, but a habit." There is nothing wrong with pursuing excellence and striving to become the best version of ourselves that we can be. Excellence is an ongoing commitment, whereas perfection acts as if it is a destination. Nothing about our success is a destination. It is a journey and a constant quest for growth and impact. We must always maintain a healthy level of humility, be able to admit our mistakes, and be willing to laugh at ourselves. The things we may be stressing about today are but a mere vapor if we look back a year from now.

QUESTIONS TO CONSIDER:

1. What does humility mean to me?
2. Where have I been holding back because of the fear of judgment from others?
3. What area of my business or life have I been overthinking?
4. What area of my business or life have I tried to be too perfect?
5. What is my primary source of energy when I need to get grounded?
6. What is one of the greatest mistakes I have made, and what did I learn from it?
7. What do I need to start doing right now, without worrying about perfection?

8. Where can I move from conscious incompetence into unconscious competence?

9. When did I try to fake it until I made it, and what was the outcome?

10. How can I live authentically and showcase my personality to others?

STOP AND COMPLETE:

Phyllis Diller said, "A smile is a curve that sets everything straight." Think back to a time in your life when you demonstrated humility. Use the space provided in your Cannonball Workbook to answer these thought-provoking questions.

1. What moment comes to mind?

2. Looking back now, was it as big of a deal as I made it out to be?

3. What unnecessary stress or anxiety did it cause me?

4. What am I able to learn from that moment?

5. How would I respond differently now if a similar moment arose?

6. What advice would I give myself back then?

CHAPTER 11

DON'T BE AFRAID OF BUMPS AND BRUISES

"Success is never final; failure is never fatal. I
t's courage to continue that counts."

WINSTON CHURCHILL

RISK IT FOR THE BISCUIT

"Inaction breeds doubt and fear. Action breeds
confidence and courage. If you want to conquer fear, do
not sit home and think about it. Go out and get busy!"

DALE CARNEGIE

To achieve success, sometimes we must throw caution to the wind and just go for it. Our goals and dreams deserve bold and decisive action. During our spring break vacation in Turks and Caicos, our youngest daughter was six years old. It was incredibly hot, and one day we were throwing a football back and forth to one another in the pool. We made each other try to dive for an incredible catch because we are both highly competitive. Out of nowhere between throws, she yells to me, "Dad, sometimes you have to risk it for the biscuit!" I paused and looked around, dumbfounded. I could not believe what she just said. Where in the world did that even come from? Did she hear it from a video she saw on YouTube? You can generally count on me for a dad joke or some cheesy quote, but I am fairly confident I never said that to my daughter.

After the shock and awe wore off and I finished laughing hysterically, I remember thinking, you know, there is a lot of wisdom packed into that statement. I began to question, what does that even mean? I concluded it serves as a reminder that our children can always teach us something, and in essence, she was reminding me that sometimes you just have to go for it! What do you want? Why do you want it? Go get it! It is simple, right? It also made me think about how we all grew up. We would dream limitless dreams of becoming an astronaut, professional athlete, teacher, veterinarian, or whatever else a kid can dream up, but then we became conditioned to hearing the word "no" so often that we became timid and complacent, accepting mediocrity or "good enough," and then letting fear overtake us. Unfortunately, for many, there is a paradigm shift that happens as we go through adulthood with more responsibilities.

This is why we created Cannonball Ventures LLC and what inspired the title of this book. It serves as a constant reminder to jump in and go for it. How do we do this? How do we reprogram our minds after years of suppressing our goals, dreams, and "go for it" attitude? In this chapter, we will discuss this and give a roadmap on how to take decisive actions that lead toward success. In the meantime, do not forget the lesson from a six-year-old—sometimes you have to risk it for the biscuit.

THE TAP ON THE SHOULDER

In late Spring of 2015, I was driving across a long stretch of bridge over Jordan Lake outside of Raleigh, North Carolina. About nine months earlier, we moved our young family into the area after living in Illinois to pursue a job opportunity. My hopes were set that this move would position our family to achieve the level of success we had desired and open a new world of opportunity for us. I also had hoped that the move would rejuvenate my energy for the CEO/team leader role I had at the time, which involved managing a large real estate office, recruiting agents into the company, and leading staff, among many other things. As I was driving over this bridge, I began to feel restless. I was looking to my right and my left, seeing all these families enjoying themselves on the boats and living the lake life. Anyone who knows me knows I am a simple man, and my dream for the longest time was to own a house on a lake. I began to question what those people did for a living and what they were doing that I was not. I began to ask, what is wrong with me? At this same time, after just moving, my family was in a mountain of debt. I was living a life like a complete fraud by pretending to my friends and family, especially on social media, that everything was perfect when behind the scenes, many things were broken. We had just liquidated my 401(k) to have cash for the big move from Illinois. We also liquidated my wife's teacher pension fund for cash. Obviously, these are retirement accounts we should not touch, but we did. Additionally, we were in $35,000 of credit card debt and owed $30,000 in back taxes.

That is when it hit me like a lightning bolt. A metaphorical tap on the shoulder or whisper in my ear that I would describe as a defining moment. I realized the restless feeling and all my unanswered questions stemmed from my not pursuing my passion. I was no longer passionate about recruiting or managing a real estate office. What lit me up like a Christmas tree was when I sat at a desk with an individual agent and could help them define their goals, create a success plan, establish their Big Why, and hold them accountable. It was at that moment that I decided to become a real estate coach. I had no idea how I would do it, but it became so clear to me. I approached my office owner, knowing there was an opening for a coaching position, but it was never offered to me. I took a behavioral assessment that said I was a ".52% medium fit" for the role of a coach. I had only sold one home in my entire career prior to obtaining a leadership position. I applied to four well-known coaching organizations and got denied every time because I did not have enough experience. None of it mattered. I knew what I was called to do. I landed the role of a productivity coach in an office in South Carolina, which required my family to move again. There was no base salary or guarantee, just an opportunity. In hindsight, from the outside looking in, it was probably very irresponsible with a young family. But I never forgot the letters I wrote to my family before we moved, and I felt called to pursue this so there were no regrets. Fast forward and in my first year as a coach, we became the number one coaching program for this international company. The Locker Room was born, and we expanded to two hundred locations within two years. In my first year as a coach, I earned more than three times what I had made any year prior to that.

The moral of the story is to take action. When we have a deep-seeded conviction and are called to do something, we must do it. I guess my daughter was right, sometimes you have to risk it for the biscuit.

LESSONS AND SUCCESS PRINCIPLES
Faith Over Fear

What is governing our decisions right now? Is it faith or fear? When success requires us to act, it is impossible not to bring up the topic of fear. Faith and fear require us to believe in something we cannot see; the choice is ours. Let's take a moment to explore fear since it can be paralyzing for so many people, which prevents them from achieving success.

What are some of the common things people are most afraid of in business?

- looking or sounding stupid
- rejection
- not knowing what to say
- judgment
- how someone else may react
- other people's opinions
- change
- failure
- uncertainty

- disappointment
- not being good enough
- success

When we examine the list above, how many of them are relatable? At some point in our life, probably all of them, if we are being honest. The good news is that we are not alone. Fear is nothing to be ashamed of or embarrassed by. Fear is not something we should pretend does not exist. It is real, normal, and shared by all. Anyone who says they do not have a fear is lying. Remember what Franklin D. Roosevelt said, "Courage is not the absence of fear, but rather the assessment that something else is more important than fear."

For example, imagine we lived thousands of years ago when Native Americans roamed the land. We were sitting in a cave with our family, and the campfire was burning to provide warmth, protection, and light. Suddenly, outside of the cave entry, we hear something in the bushes moving around. We look at our family questioning what is making the noise outside of the cave. At that moment, our fight or flight mechanism has taken over. We have a choice to act in faith or retreat in fear. We do not know if the animal making the sound is going to try to eat us or if we are going to eat it for dinner. Fear is primitive to all of us. Fear is innate to who we are because we are human beings filled with emotions and feelings. Fear is not foreign or something we need to pretend does not exist. The reality is that fear is a protection mechanism. Fear is actually a good thing, and it is meant to serve us.

The next time we experience fear, let's personify it. Have a conversation with the fear, no differently than we would another person. For example, a real estate agent knows their success is dependent upon picking up the phone and calling people to lead-generate. The problem is, when they look at the phone or even think about dialing someone, they become paralyzed in fear. Using this example, personify fear by having a conversation that might sound like this: "Hello, Fear, good to see you again. Listen, I know you are here trying to protect me, and I really appreciate that. Here is the thing, I am going to be okay. I am going to call my friend to see if I can be of any help to them, and I know my friend would appreciate hearing from me today. I will take it from here, but thanks again for always trying to protect me. Until next time..."

If we confront our fear, rather than trying to pretend it does not exist or even feel embarrassed by it, then we will liberate ourselves and be more capable of taking the actions necessary to achieve our goals. Some people may say that fear is a liar, or it is false evidence appearing real. I understand the nature of the saying, but as a realist, I would rather say fear is actually not a liar. Fear is a good thing, and it is on my side to serve and protect. In some ways, it is a governing authority to make sure I am kept safe, no different than the true men and women in police uniforms who are out there to protect and serve. When confronting fear, we may have considerations we ask, such as, what is the worst that can happen? Have we ever asked ourselves, what is the best thing that could happen, instead? Why do we always resort to the negative rather than the positive?

According to a research article published in 2005, Robert W. Schrauf, an associate professor of applied linguistics at Penn State, asked groups of people in Mexico City and Chicago in two age groups, twenty years old and sixty-five years old, to list the names of as many emotions as they could. The emotions were then categorized as negative, positive, or neutral. The exercise concluded, "People know more negative emotion words than positive or neutral words. The proportion of words was fifty percent negative, thirty percent positive, and twenty percent neutral," says Schrauf. "The cognitive explanation is that we process negative and positive emotions in two channels." [13] Subsequently, it was cited in another report in an issue of the Journal of Multilingual and Multicultural Development, "the researchers explain that positive emotions are processed schematically. People do not pay a lot of attention to the assessment of positive emotions. In general, positive emotions signal that things are okay, so we process them more superficially. Negative emotions signal that something is wrong, and so they elicit a slowdown in processing. They require more attention and detail in thinking and, consequently, more words." [14]

Knowing this lets us understand that we are not alone and, in fact, it is quite normal. Our minds are wired to be in constant survival mode, and the emotion of fear is the protection mechanism to let us know that something is not familiar, and we should process it. However, just like anything, the more we do something, the less scary it gets. In fact, we become quite good at it with more repetition and it becomes easy. Let's step up to the plate with confidence next time we experience fear. In the words of Suzy Kassem, "Fear kills more dreams than failure ever will."

To help you calculate the risk and reward of taking action compared to not taking action, there is a well-known model leaders use called the Pain vs. Gain model. I first learned of the Pain vs. Gain model through Tony Robbins. The Pain vs. Gain model asks you to answer the following questions in order, any time you are struggling to decide or act due to fear:

1. How is the current situation causing pain? (Current Pain)
2. What is to be gained from making the change? (Future Gain)

3. What is the benefit of the current situation? (Current Gain)

4. How might the change cause pain? (Future Pain)

This is a very simple model to help you do a cost-benefit analysis. You can view a 360-degree image of the situation and leverage the perspective it gives you. I have used this countless times in my coaching career, and the awareness and discussions it creates help people analyze their situation for what it is and then determine the best course of action moving forward.

Speed of Implementation

If you have ever seen the movie *Forrest Gump*,[15] you are likely familiar with the scene where Jenny yells, "Run Forest, Run!" That set Forest in motion to run all across the United States, inspiring thousands of people. In the words of Forest Gump, when asked why he was running across the country, he said, "I just felt like running." Although it is a scene in a movie, how many metaphorical scenes like that play out in our lives? When taking action, the speed of implementation is undoubtedly one of the greatest success principles I have discovered. Do not take it from me, listen to Tom Cruise in the movie *Top Gun*[16] when he said, "I feel the need, the need for speed." Speed equals acceleration. Our success requires us to push the throttle forward and move with acceleration.

Succeeding in business and life requires us to take action. No textbook prepares us for the lessons life will give us. Experience is the best teacher, and experience is a result of action. If we do nothing, then we will get nothing. If we do something, we will achieve something. I know this sounds elementary, but we cannot be so quick to label what the "something" is. It is neither good nor bad; it just is.

Experience is the mother of all teachers, and through taking action, we are guaranteed to learn something if we are willing to reflect. We can choose to put ourselves on the path to earning our doctorate for success in record time if we apply speed of implementation. To prevent us from slowing down, it is critical to accept one thing, and that is our willingness to fail forward. Every step is not going to be perfect, and we are going to trip and fall over ourselves along the way. We will get bumps, bruises, and scrapes from challenges we never saw coming, but that is much better than running straight into a wall because we tried to take a shortcut. There are no shortcuts.

One of the core principles I communicate in my coaching business is that it takes ninety days to create or lose momentum. What you do today will show up in ninety days. Similarly, what you are not doing today will also show up in the lack of results ninety days from now. In business there are certain success principles that apply even when we do not see them. No different than gravity, I do not need to see gravity to know it exists. The same is true for creating momentum. We have already acknowledged that success behaviors can be boring, repetitious, and mundane. The last thing some people need is more information. Knowledge is just stored information; knowledge is not necessarily power unless applied. To assist with this, here is a formula for success we can consider when applying speed of implementation to create momentum:

- **Get clear on what we want.** Whatever we look at with our eyes, whether open or closed, our mind will recognize it and work to make it happen. We have an opportunity to train our nervous system so the brain, the body, and our emotions cannot tell what is real if we vividly imagine it. Where our attention goes, our energy flows.

- **Know our reasons why.** We talked about this in Chapter 1. Knowing *what* we want does not mean we will be in alignment with the reason *why* we want it. Procrastination, hesitation, and doubt are the thieves of dreams. The why comes first, and the how comes second. We will do the first step out of intuitiveness because we know what we want. When we establish why we want it, we will be pulled toward it even when we do not feel like taking action.

- **Take immediate action.** Execute immediate, massive, and consistent action, so we develop muscle memory just like working out in the gym.

- **Pay attention to what we are accomplishing.** Check-in and reflect frequently. What are we learning? What can we do better? What adjustments need to be made? Utilize the K.I.S.S. questions.

- **Change our approach.** Adjust by studying game film and improving for next time. Pay attention and ask powerful questions.

To help take improved action and provide some perspective, answer the following questions in the space provided in your Cannonball Workbook:

1. When was there a time in my life when I was at the pinnacle of performance and experienced huge success?

   What were my daily habits that led to my success?

   What was my mindset like?

   Who did I spend the most time with?

2. When was there a time in my life when I was not performing well and experienced frustration, stress, and anxiety?

> What were my self-sabotaging habits?

> What was my mindset like?

> Who did I spend the most time with?

3. What are the key differences between those two experiences?

4. Which actions am I exhibiting right now? What actions am I committed to doing, moving forward?

Going Full Throttle: Creating Momentum

Most people fail to achieve their goals in life because they never take the first step. Here are five simple steps to begin creating momentum.

Step 1: Put yourself in the right frame of mind. Listen to music, go workout, or talk to a mentor. The goal is to ensure your mind is ready to take on the moment.

Step 2: Be passionate! As Brian Tracy says, "Sales is the transfer of enthusiasm." What do you love? What gives you the most energy? What are you passionate about? What do value the most? When are you operating in your strength zone? Make sure you are congruent in all ways.

Step 3: Decide and commit. You must be unwavering, unapologetic, and borderline obsessive with your resolve. Put your armor on and go into battle.

Step 4: Take immediate, smart, and consistent action. Follow a proven model of success and execute it flawlessly. Time on task over time will always win. Consistency is still undefeated.

Step 5: Use S.M.A.R.T. goals. Execute your strategy and then check it, change it, reengineer it, and reinforce it. Know the scoreboard and what game you are playing. Measure results often, assess what is working and not, then reinforce what works and take improved action to continue the momentum.

Earn the Nickname

In 2017, I earned the nickname of "T.O.T.O.T" by one of the real estate agents I was coaching. Apparently, I said, "time on task over time" so many times that he decided to give me that acronym as a nickname. What time on task over time allows is not just consistency, but more so, it allows us the opportunity to see what works and what doesn't. The ability to make in-game adjustments results in us taking improved action. After we have reached a level of consistency with our actions, we have learned to embrace our fears and turn them into constructive energy. We have adopted speed of implementation that leads to momentum, and now we can modify our activities for improved action since we have a history of behaviors to study. As they say, the definition of insanity is doing the same thing over and over and expecting a different result. It is important to make the distinction here between action and improved action. By now, we have analytics to study with a track record of results, so we can formulate key performance indicators by chunking things down.

Chunking is the ability to take something that may be complex and break it down piece by piece. For example, I coached a husband-and-wife real estate team from 2016 to 2018. From the first day we began working together, they consistently tracked their numbers and reported them to me for accountability. Over time, we could observe common patterns and trends that lead us to take improved action. After more than two years of coaching together, we knew that for every twenty-nine conversations they had it would result in one new appointment with a buyer or seller client. We also knew that for every forty-eight conversations it would yield them one new contract written. Based on averages, their annual income goal required them to go on seven appointments per month and have five closings. With the data we had over an extended period, it allowed us to make educated assumptions. Knowing every twenty-nine conversations resulted in an appointment allowed us to apply basic math by taking 29 x 7, totaling 203 conversations for the month. Their closed unit goal of five per month allowed us to take forty-eight conversations x 5, which totals 240 conversations. Every month this meant they needed a range from 203 to 240 conversations to stay on pace for their goal.

No matter how busy they got, they needed to chunk things down granularly to keep the leading indicators on pace to consistently hit their lagging indicators. If that is not impressive enough, we even chunked things down to assess the average value of a conversation. Their average commission was about $6,000 per closing. If we go back to the original forty-eight conversations for one new piece of business, then we divided $6,000 by 48 and it told us the average value of a contact was $125. By knowing this information, the agents could remove emotion from the equation and begin operating as CEOs. They knew that if they spoke to ten people per day, they just made $1,250. It may not have shown up in their bank account yet, but in their mind, they connected the activity to a result and had faith that the leading indicators would yield the desired results.

None of this could have happened without consistency and chunking things down.

Given the data set, now we could take improved action. They proved they were consistent. They proved they were operating their business like a business by knowing their numbers. We did not have to worry about that any longer, so now, we could shift the attention to increased efficiency and skillset. At the time, their conversion rate for buyers was about fifty-two percent, and their conversion rate for sellers was seventy-three percent. Instead of working harder, we set out to work smarter. How could we achieve the same goal but reduce the number of contacts necessary? The answer was to improve their conversion rates. We focused on improving the buyer conversion rate to get as high as their seller conversion rate. To do so, we analyzed their actions, systems, and standards. We found they were rushing out to show buyers property without properly pre-qualifying them. We implemented new standards and systems while keeping the activities consistent, and we got their buyer conversion rate up by over seventy percent. This is a perfect example of what it means to take improved action. The answer does not always lie in working harder. If we know the proper set of data to track and apply time on task over time, the numbers begin to tell a story. What are some key metrics in our career that we need to know at all times? If we are in sales, some of those may include the number of attempts to a contact, the number of contacts to an appointment, the number of appointments to a contract written, the number of contracts written to a closing, and the number of closings necessary to achieve our desired income.

Do not be fooled by the simplicity. It is simple disciplines repeated over time that result in success. Growing up, we heard the doctor tell us that an apple per day would keep the doctor away. The doctor did not say to eat seven apples on Sunday. He said an apple per day.

Have we ever considered the wisdom in that? To illustrate the point, think about the "trick question" someone may have asked: would you rather have $1,000,000 cash right now, or would you rather begin with a penny that doubles every day for thirty consecutive days? The temptation for most is to take the $1,000,000 cash. The reason is because it is instant gratification. We can see it, and it is guaranteed. However, with patience and the compound effect, by day thirty, we will have made $5,368,709.12 all by starting with a single penny and the amount doubling every day for thirty consecutive days. However, it is important to note that it is all about the power of doubling with the compound effect because if we asked the same question but changed the amount of time to twenty-seven days, then we would only have $671,088.64. Are we willing to take improved action and apply time on task over time? Unfortunately, many are on the edge of achieving success; yet, they pull up short, begin questioning things, and stop their activities, so they never realize the breakthrough waiting for them.

Sweat the Small Stuff

We have likely heard the saying, "Do not sweat the small stuff," and in the right context, I tend to agree. However, when it comes to taking action, I strongly disagree. The devil is in the details regarding our actions. Assuming we are taking measured and accountable action, remember to always celebrate the small victories along the way. We have spoken about recognition and how it is necessary regardless of what our behavior style is. After coaching thousands of professionals, it is common to see them discount their small victories along the way to achieving their big victories. It is time to sweat the small stuff and give ourselves permission to celebrate.

I used to coach a 12U baseball team in Florida. During the first practice of the season, I would get the kids together and paint a picture. I would tell them to close their eyes and imagine the league president interrupting our practice with a five-foot trophy in hand. The league president walks up to us and says, "Congratulations, you won the league!" For several minutes, I am sure everyone would jump for joy and celebrate, but I cannot help but think after several minutes, everyone would pause and ask questions. We would ask how it was possible that we won the entire championship without playing a single game, let alone one practice. It is possible we would not even want the trophy or feel worthy of holding it, once given time to process things. That is because much of our success also lies in appreciating the journey. It is the sacrifices, blood, sweat, and tears that go into achieving success. The journey is just as important as the destination. Trophies and money can be earned and lost, but the person we become while achieving success can never be taken away.

For this reason, we need to sweat the small stuff. Do not take the process for granted. In some ways, we must marry the process and divorce the results. Massive success is simply a combination of many little victories that lead to one big victory, so why discount them along the way? We have permission to celebrate and allow ourselves to set milestones, and when we reach a milestone, we go out to a nice dinner or treat ourselves to a reward. Our affirmations along the way will only empower us further toward our ultimate definition of success. If a child was doing great in school, wouldn't we find ways to reward the behavior we would like to see more often? In grade school, our oldest daughter earned an award that was voted on by her peers. The award was for respect, responsibility, safety, and being a good friend. It was the coveted award all kids strived to earn in the school, and she earned it for two consecutive years. My wife and I were incredibly proud of her and went out of our way to celebrate the behavior we wanted to see more of. We knew winning that award was not the end all be all in the big picture, but it certainly was a leading indicator to raising a daughter we were proud of. By the way, her choice for the award was going to Qdoba for dinner, so we got off pretty cheap.

Habit vs. Rhythm

> "Change the way you look at things and the things you look at change."
>
> **WAYNE DYER**

When taking productive action, most people know what to do; they just fight themselves against doing it. Do not get me wrong, I very much value habits and agree with many leaders who say that success lies in our daily habits. Yet, what if there was another element we have not considered or given enough attention to? What if we created consistent and meaningful action with half of the equation? What if the other half of the equation was creating a *rhythm*? This realization hit me when listening to an audiobook called *The Family Board Meeting*[17] by Jim Sheils. Sheils mentioned how he does not think of things in terms of *habits*. He proceeded to explain how it felt restrictive and task-oriented. He used an example that serves as the basis of his book that his goal was to get in a *rhythm* with his children where every ninety days, he held a "family board meeting" with each one by taking them out to do something fun. No technology was involved, only focused attention on one another to create memories.

This got me thinking about the relationship we have with ourselves, our calendars, our friends, our clients, and how we approach success in general. For example, we are fed a lot of information when it comes to time management and habits but something about the rhythm perspective triggered me. I began to consider how this may apply to my experiences or common occurrences that I could relate to. I thought about the game of baseball. Nearly every lesson I would give to a kid while running my indoor baseball training facility included the word rhythm. I was a student of the game and always stressed the importance of staying loose. Many parents yell from the bleachers, "Get your back elbow up! Keep your eye on the ball! Swing hard!" Aside from mechanics, I would instruct my players to not think about swinging hard. When a player thinks this way, then they grip the bat tighter, and you can see their white knuckles and forearms completely stiff. Every muscle in their body tenses when I want them to be loose and relaxed.

Our words matter, so rather than telling my players to swing hard, I would tell them to be quick. Have quick wrists and fast bat speed to hit the ball with power. It was no different when they were standing in the batter's box waiting for the pitcher to throw. We will see kids standing there like statues, almost as if they were frozen. I instructed my players to have some rhythm in the batter's box—small and quiet movements that allow them to stay loose and establish a rhythm. After all, hitting is all about timing, and pitching is all about disrupting a hitter's timing, so it was important they stay loose and establish a rhythm so their timing would be more aligned with the pitcher. The mechanics of their swing were important to have good habits and fundamental mechanics to tick all the checkpoints. However, once the ball is delivered and the batter gets ready to swing, the habits become more about muscle memory through training and repetition.

As the ball is released, we are either ready by having a fundamentally sound swing, or we aren't. It becomes all about rhythm and timing for the batter from there, which is why I believe there is a second aspect to taking action, and all of the focus is not just on establishing proper habits. We need a rhythm that moves us towards our success combined with the proper success habits.

When I think of the difference between rhythm and habits, I think of how rhythm creates a mental image of the "whole" working as one, all connected, and in unison. It makes me think of a natural flow or fluid motion, like a Major League batter crushing a home run. Everything was timed right, and the swing seemed to flow effortlessly rather than rigid and separate from every stage of his swing. Rhythm makes me think of not overanalyzing, but rather, involuntary movements that allow us to be fully present in the moment. Rhythm makes me think of being comfortable and making something effortless. One of the best compliments a coach can give a player in any sport is how they make things look effortless. They have practiced and applied time on task over time so that muscle memory takes over, and the motion becomes second nature. In terms of energy, when I think of rhythm, I think of positive energy. In fact, it gives me energy. Whereas, when I think of habits, it can be draining or something you "have to do" and not look forward to. Perhaps this is where things such as "get comfortable being uncomfortable" are born, as we spoke about previously because we are trying to force habits.

Rhythm is a sequence, whereas a habit has a defined start and finish time on a calendar. I think of rhythm as being more athletic and agile compared to a habit being potentially forced and robotic. It is easy to go through the motions with a habit, whereas a rhythm forces us to be in tune with ourselves, aware of our movements, and aligned so all parts work together. Aristotle said himself, "The whole is greater than the sum of its parts." What is the underlying principle? If we look at how we approach our days, what if we reframed how they should flow seamlessly together rather than a series of tasks that stop and start separately? Remember, when we change how we look at things, the things we look at change. Rather than focusing on habits, what if we thought of it as a rhythm? For example, let's consider some of the following questions:

- What is my rhythm when it comes to lead generation?
- What is my rhythm when it comes to building relationships?
- What is my rhythm when working with a customer?
- What is my rhythm when it comes to family life?
- What is my rhythm in the morning?
- What is my rhythm before bed?

What kind of energy do we feel when we ask those questions and replace the word habit with rhythm? For me, it seems more harmonious and easy-flowing, like the batter who should swing quickly with loose wrists rather than gripping the bat so hard with white knuckles that he is too tense even to make contact. It's like someone who works out consistently and says if they miss a single day, then it throws the rest of the day off. I will use my sister as an example. Her days are set up with a rhythm. Every morning, she runs several miles. If she does not get her running in, the rhythm of her day is completely off, and she is less productive since the rhythm was disrupted. It is not a *habit* for her to run several miles per day; it is part of her daily rhythm. What if we got to that point with an activity in our life that we knew directly impacted our success? If we are in sales, what if our lead generation becomes a rhythm in our day that disrupts our entire day if we do not do it? Something would feel off about the rest of the day if we missed a day. Instead of being a time-blocked habit, what if it was just a part of our daily rhythm?

For example, I am a big proponent of "life styling" for lead generation. In other words, consider what we do on any normal day and find ways to generate business around that instead of thinking we must be sitting behind a cubicle and making calls for three consecutive hours. Life styling may include taking kids to school, picking them up from school, attending community events, grocery shopping, running into the post office, or any other activity that is a natural part of our daily rhythm. We can simply take our everyday flow and rhythm of life and incorporate intentional business conversations with those we encounter, so it is not a forced habit but rather something that feels natural. Establish success habits that can be developed into a rhythm. Once we achieve a state of flow, our path to success will seem effortless and not forced. We become the person who deserves the success we seek rather than checking items off a daily habit checklist.

Puppy Dog Eyes and Pouty Lips

No chapter on taking action would be complete without addressing the obvious. Our children are expert negotiators and put on a clinic for us when it comes to being persistent. Persistence itself is undoubtedly one of the most important success principles as it relates to taking action. Like most parents, I have numerous examples of our children out-maneuvering me to get what they want.

> *"Can I have this toy? Please, please, please."*

> *"Will you play Roblox with me? Please, please, please."*

> *"Will you go outside and play with me? Please, please, please."*

Those are not questions repeated once. Those questions are repeated hundreds of times, if necessary, until they get what they want and wear me down till I finally say yes. Children are relentless when it comes to getting what they want. In most cases, if persistence is not enough, it is generally followed with sweet puppy dog eyes and a pouty lip sticking out that makes it impossible to say no. We can all relate to this in some way. However, when was the last time we paused to consider the success principle that they are teaching us? Are we asking for what we want? Are we persistent enough, assuming we want it badly? To achieve success, we must be determined to reach the goal and yet flexible in our approach. Four years into building our real estate coaching company, I questioned whether we were on the right track. We had made so many pivots and adjustments along the way that I began to question myself and if I was even a good leader. I wondered if great leaders made as many mistakes as I was making. I wondered if I was not being intentional enough. I wondered if our coaches and clients would leave the company because it seemed like I was always changing something. I read a passage in a training manual I had received a few years prior. In this manual, it said, "Historically, five-plus reinventions will be necessary to get you to your desired levels of success. The lack of comprehending this reinvention reality and then living it is the number one reason for failure or mediocre success."

I needed to hear those words at that exact time. I remember feeling relieved that I was not alone and in fact, constant reinvention was all part of the process. It could be argued that if I were not constantly analyzing things and adjusting, it would contribute to a collapse in the business. In other words, the constant adaptation and reinvention ended up being the reason we were still growing and not the reason that others would think to leave. Building a business is incredibly hard. Growth is messy and we must anticipate constant reinvention while pursuing our goals. Do not be afraid of the mess; embrace it. Focus on the goals, ask for what is wanted, and persist relentlessly.

In real estate coaching, we developed a challenge-concept for real estate agents to grow their businesses in a manner requiring persistence and time on task over time. We called the challenge the "5 to 25 Challenge." The Challenge shows agents a mathematical formula to achieve twenty-five additional sales per year. We challenge real estate agents to have five conversations per day, five days a week, for fifty weeks out of the year. By doing so, they will have had 1,250 real estate conversations over the course of a single year. For many years, we have monitored the traditional conversation rates for newer and less experienced real estate agents, and we commonly find a 50:1 ratio. Meaning that for every fifty conversations, it will yield one new piece of business. Therefore, with our challenge, agents can follow a mathematical formula for success by speaking with five people daily. The compound effect when time on task over time and persistency is applied cannot be stopped. Of course, there will be days when all we hear is the word no. The goal is not to earn business through every conversation but to persist and do the right activity long enough so the law of averages can appear. To quote a passage out of *The Traveler's Gift*,[18] Andy Andrews writes, "How long must a child try to walk before he actually does so? Do I not have more strength than a child, more understanding, more desire? How long must I work to succeed before I actually do so? A child would never ask the question for the answer does not matter. By persisting without exception, my outcome, my success is assured."

QUESTIONS TO CONSIDER:

1. What milestones do I need to set for myself?

2. In what ways will I celebrate my small victories?

3. What aspect of my career do I need to apply more time on task over time?

4. Where am I currently being impatient to see results?

5. What key indicators do I need to begin tracking to take improved action?

6. What fear am I holding onto that I need to address?

7. What have I been putting off that requires me to take action right now?

8. How has delayed action cost me opportunities in the past?

9. How am I going to build momentum towards success?

10. What action can I take to accelerate my learning through experience, right now?

STOP AND COMPLETE:

This chapter would not be complete without finishing where we started. It is your time to risk it for the biscuit. Complete the following exercise in your Cannonball Workbook, which were inspired by our youngest daughter. Remember, you deserve all the success in the world, so throw caution to the wind and go get what is yours.

CHAPTER 12

NO TRAFFIC JAMS HERE

"Sometimes letting go is an act of far greater
power than defending or hanging on."

ECKHART TOLLE

LEAVE IT ALL OUT ON THE PLAYGROUND

Our youngest daughter came home visibly upset one day from elementary school. Curious to know what happened, my wife sat her down in her room and asked what was wrong. Our daughter proceeded to tell her how one of her closest friends kept tackling her during recess and how she wished that she would stop. She had never dealt with anything like this before and was too scared to say anything to her close friend out of fear that she would be mad. My wife was able to calm her down and work toward an agreeable solution that our daughter felt comfortable with. The resolution was that we would email her teacher and ask her to please watch closely at recess and, if she saw it happen, to please help intervene. Additionally, our daughter felt comfortable writing a note to her friend and handing it to her the next day at school. The note basically said how she did not like to be tackled because it made her sad and to please stop.

The next day at school went without incident. The friend apologized, and the teacher never had to intervene. Since then, there has been no tackling on the playground during recess. This was not a case of bullying but rather taking things a little too far while playing together. Her friend did not want our daughter to play with other kids, and every time she tried to, the friend would tackle her to prevent her from playing with anyone else. After the incident was resolved, I began to think of the principle that could be extracted. As Margaret Thatcher said, "Disciplining yourself to do what you know is right and important, although difficult, is the high road to pride, self-esteem, and personal satisfaction." I was proud of our daughter for speaking out and doing what was right. She rose above the situation instead of retaliating by doing or saying something she might regret later. Our daughter was able to get through the rest of the day, express her emotions at home, and then find a solution to make things better in the future. Is that not textbook?

As we journey through success, we will face many challenges and opportunities to say things out of frustration in the moment. The playground bully will show up, and we will question whether or not to exchange punches. We will be tempted to lose our temper or react to others out of emotion rather than responding in a high-minded manner. The ability to take the high road builds character, and there are no traffic jams on the high road. We don't have to fall victim to others by lowering our standards to meet their approval. Or, as

Wayne Dyer would say, "How people treat you is their karma. How you react is yours."

KEEP LEADING WITH THE HEART

One of the most challenging times of my business career was between 2017 and 2019. We were experiencing rapid growth in our business, The Locker Room. Since expanding in July 2017, within the first two years, we created a platform used by two hundred real estate offices across North America. While the growth was amazing, the obstacles and headwinds we faced behind the scenes were anything but. It began when I received a random email from a C-level executive within the company I was affiliated with. The email was very short and to the point, stating that this individual would like to set up a call with me to learn more about our business. At the time, this international company had their own internal coaching company and yet there was no system or model like the one I had built for other coaches. Naturally, they wanted to learn more, but this was the day I had expected would come. I remember my palms being sweaty in anticipation of the phone call we had scheduled. After we spoke, there was a mutual understanding, and we were able to proceed under certain conditions, which I had continuously upheld. Over time, we continued to grow and create more buzz within the organization. The phone calls and emails grew in frequency, and the friction became stronger. Through their lens, I created a competing coaching company that was taking business away from the company-owned coaching company.

I remember being at a live training event in San Antonio, Texas, and I received a text from this individual. They stated that they knew I was in attendance and wanted to meet during one of the breaks. The next day, I approached the individual during a short break, and we had a chance to speak. They told me they have been talking a lot about The Locker Room and wanted to find a way to fold it into their coaching company. Short on time, the individual instructed me to email them later that night with what it would take financially to explore this option. When I got to my hotel room, I sent the email, but I never approached the subject of money. I had a lot of questions that first needed to be answered, and I was not willing to sell out my team just for the sake of money.

My questions never got answered, and things turned south very quickly from there. I became the outcast and was asked to fly to headquarters to meet with the leadership team. I did so willingly and never was combative. I was always forthcoming with information about my intentions and even showed them all the tools we had created. I was an open book with nothing to hide. One Monday morning, I remember receiving a phone call from the owner of a region in Florida that had twelve offices utilizing our company. In one phone call, we lost all twelve because they stated how the individual I had been meeting with instructed them that they could not have our business as a part of their offices. This was the final straw. It was clear that the company I was with was doing everything in its power to prohibit our growth. The writing was on the wall that they were only tolerating me and not willing to celebrate with me. Not for a moment did I consider myself a victim. I knew everything happened for a reason and would reveal itself to me one day.

That day came when I needed it the most. I attended a Tony Robbins event in Chicago, and one of the exercises helped me dig deep into my mindset to work through many frustrations and anxieties I was having through all of this. At the end of the exercise, I wrote: "Keep leading with your heart, and everything is going to be okay." Those are the words I needed to hear myself say. I could not control the attitudes or actions of others, but I was in control of mine. I knew we were operating out of integrity and had a platform that could help a lot of people. I could not and would not apologize for that. From that day forward, I decided to leave that company and become brand-agnostic. Ever since then, we have worked with hundreds of real estate companies and helped tens of thousands of real estate agents. Whether it is our daughter on the playground or my own experiences, one thing is for certain: success requires us to take the high road even when we are tempted not to. We must keep a level head, operate with integrity, and drown out the noise. Steve Jobs was right, "Don't let the noise of others' opinions drown out your own inner voice."

LESSONS AND SUCCESS PRINCIPLES
The Platinum Rule

The Golden Rule says, "Do unto others as you would have them do unto you." Essentially, this means treating others how you want to be treated. Tony Alessandra and Michael O'Connor wrote a book called The Platinum Rule,[19] and they proposed, "Do unto others as 'they would' like done unto them." In other words, treat others how they want to be treated.

A breakthrough moment occurred in 2016 when I fully understood this concept. I was establishing my footing as a new real estate coach and had interviewed sixty-two other coaches who were in the same role I had just been hired for. I asked them about their approach to coaching real estate agents, the frequency of meetings, the content they taught, and how they conducted one-on-one meetings. After interviewing sixty-two different coaches, I learned of sixty-one ways

I knew I did not want to run my coaching business. Nothing against them, but it was all robotic and impersonal. I wanted to be different, and their methods gave me a glimpse of what I did not want to do, which ultimately helped me establish what I did. I created a program directly opposite of what most were doing. I used the guiding principle that people do not care how much you know until they know how much you care. While everyone else was doing group coaching sessions to leverage time, I met with agents one-on-one instead. While others made their real estate agents earn a one-on-one coaching session, I gave every agent in my program two monthly one-on-one sessions by default.

When I interviewed other coaches, asking them why they did not meet with agents one-on-one unless they hit a production level, their responses were generally self-absorbed. I heard things like them not wanting to meet with every new agent because the successful ones would make it, and everyone else was unmotivated and would not. I heard them justify their time because they were busy, and the agents should be grateful for the group sessions offered. Every conversation I had created more clarity that if I was going to succeed, I had to do things completely opposite. That started with treating people how they wanted to be treated. I thought, if I was in their shoes, what would I want my coach to do for me? When I could place myself in their shoes, I created a value proposition with them in mind rather than putting myself in the center. To achieve success, it is important to put ourselves in the shoes of another person. I realized it required a high sense of discernment and empathy towards others. Henry Ford was right when he said, "If there is any one secret of success, it lies in the ability to get the other person's point of view and see things from his angle as well as your own."

Taking the high road requires us to understand *The Platinum Rule* and remove ourselves from the situation no matter how hard it may be. Our words and actions have consequences. I can think of times when a close friend or someone I respected said things to me in a moment of anger that they probably did not mean. Most of the time, I do not remember the exact words they said, but I distinctly remember how it made me feel. Maya Angelou said, "At the end of the day, people won't remember what you said or did, they will remember how you made them feel." She is absolutely right.

When we encounter a potential conflict, a moment of anger, or have someone do something to us that warrants revenge, pause. Remember *The Platinum Rule* and the words of Maya Angelou. Success requires us to rise above the noise and not lower our standards. Success requires us to understand conflict resolution, remove our emotions from the equation, and immediately get into logic. When mentioning conflict resolution, there are five key steps to follow.

1. **Define the source of the conflict.** Get to the root of the issue rather than trying to put a bandage on the problem. For example, we may ask questions such as: "When did you feel upset?" or "What is the real issue?" or "How did this happen?"

2. **Look beyond the conflict to gain perspective.** It is often not the event that triggered someone, but rather the interpretation or perception of it. It is the gap between expectation and reality that may upset someone. Typically, this is from anger and resentment building over time and then boiling over. So although a minor incident may have occurred to create a conflict, odds are there is more to the story. If we are involved in the situation, it is best to ask

questions and listen rather than state our opinion, which will only complicate the problem. A common way of saying this is to seek first to understand and then be understood.

3. **Shift to focusing on solutions.** After gaining perspective, get in solution mode. We may ask questions such as, "What would you like to see done differently?" or "How can we work past this to an agreeable outcome?" Asking solution-based questions is critical to becoming an active listener. Being an active listener is not just the words but also observing tonality, body language, and what they are not saying.

4. **Create a win-win solution.** Every conflict requires compromise. Cooler heads will prevail if they feel valued and heard and have a clear direction to move forward. We are listening for the most acceptable course of action. As possible solutions are presented, we can point out the merits of various ideas, especially those that are mutually beneficial of the benefits to the organization.

5. **Agreement.** The final step is to reach a mutual agreement in which everyone feels valued, heard, and respected. This should benefit the relationship, the organization, or the success of each other.

Reading this may cause us to feel like we are a counselor. In many ways, that's not wrong. We are human beings with feelings, emotions, and desires. Deep conviction and passion are not negative things if we show empathy and seek to understand the perspectives of others. *The Platinum Rule* keeps us in check that we treat others how they want to be treated rather than feeling they should adapt to us. Knowing these basic principles allows us to see past any moment of conflict and take the high road, which our success depends on.

Rise Above the Noise

During adversity, people will pay more attention to what we do rather than what we say. Napoleon Hill famously said, "Out of resistance comes strength." When our character comes into question or when conflict arises, it can be very tempting to let our guard down and easier to succumb to the temptation of getting in the ring with someone. However, real strength comes from demonstrating restraint rather than sparring with someone else.

Prior to going to college in 2001 to play baseball, I had never consistently lifted weights to improve my strength. I was successful simply based on my work ethic and natural abilities but had a large upside given my tall frame. In my first year of college, I gained twenty-five pounds just by being dedicated to the weight room and implementing resistance training into my routine. It was my junior year when I tore my pitching elbow ligament and had surgery. Prior to the injury, I threw eighty-eight to ninety miles per hour as a pitcher. During rehabilitation, I had to perform more resistance training than I ever did before. I was constantly in the weight room working with our athletic training staff to build back the strength in my pitching arm. After rehab, I remember being clocked at ninety-four miles per hour. I was the same size but this time, I had more strength and conditioning to specific muscle groups in my arm than I had previously.

When we lift weights, we experience fatigue and soreness. The soreness stems from small tears in our muscles, which rebuild, making us stronger than before. The short-term downside or soreness is temporary, but in the long run, the resistance makes us stronger. The same is true for our journey of success. We are going to get sore from time to time. It may not be our muscles, but perhaps it's our emotions, our will, our adaptation to a change, or a new rhythm we are introduced to. The metaphorical soreness may be from undergoing more resistance than ever before. Yet, it is the resistance that will make us stronger and capable of taking on more in the end. To be a leader of others, we must be a leader of ourselves first. To lift others up, we must be able to lift ourselves up first. The next time we experience soreness we can recognize it is likely because of the resistance that is not only building our muscles to lift ourselves up but also others toward success along the way. James N. Wakins said, "A river cuts through a rock not because of its power but because of its persistence."

As we set out toward achieving our goals, we must expect resistance, anticipate it will be harder than we think, take more time, and require more resources. We can prepare ourselves for the mental, physical, and emotional battles we may encounter while pursuing success. When it shows up, we can understand we are being tested and associate it with resistance training, just as if we were in the gym building muscle. When we do this, we will be stronger to handle the skeptics, critics, and roadblocks that try to prevent us from achieving our goals. Remember, as previously stated, just because someone gave up on their goals does not mean they have permission to talk us out of ours. There are no traffic jams when we take the high road.

> "If your actions inspire others to dream more, learn more, do more, and become more, you are a leader."
>
> **JOHN QUINCY ADAMS**

QUESTIONS TO CONSIDER:

1. How do I traditionally approach handling conflict?
2. What conversation have I been putting off that I need to have right now?
3. How will I handle things when someone challenges my goals?
4. How can I apply the Platinum Rule in my relationships?
5. What impact would seeking first to understand have on my success rather than passing judgment?
6. Where have I built resentment, and how can I find a solution, so I do not carry that negative energy around any longer?
7. How do I handle adversity?
8. What is my first reaction when someone says I cannot do something?
9. When was a time in my life that I intentionally chose to take the high road?
10. Who can I express gratitude toward that has impacted me due to having high standards and consistently taking the high road?

STOP AND COMPLETE:

Right now, you are probably experiencing negative resistance in some aspect of your work or life. The byproduct of negative resistance can be frustration, and the longer you hold onto it, the more it works against you rather than for you. In this exercise, identify your frustration and work through it to identify a solution in your Cannonball Workbook. Although you are only doing this for one frustration, the process can be applied to others you may also be feeling. It is time to starve your frustration by taking the high road and being solution-based.

A NOTE FROM THE AUTHOR

Thank you for going on this journey toward success with me. By no means do I pretend to have this whole thing figured out. In fact, I am sure that after publishing this book, I will have plenty of new stories, perspectives, and principles I could share. Life is a journey, and none of us will make it out alive. You deserve to do what you love, surround yourself with people who lift you up, and pursue *your* definition of success.

Every game, before our college baseball team took the field, our coach would get us in a huddle and say, "Have fun, stick together, and play like champions." I can close my eyes now and hear his words perfectly. Children provide us the perspective to have fun and never lose sight of the child-like faith that is in all of us. They remind us of the importance of family and the strength of sticking together. Children demand us to show up as champions because they look to us for strong leadership. Whatever I may or may not accomplish in business, I chalk this book up as one of my greatest accomplishments. It has been a passion project of mine and a gift I can pass on to generations. I cannot thank you enough for supporting my family and me by reading this book, and I hope you found value in doing so.

From here, the work has just begun. You did not come this far to only come this far. Once you achieve success, it is your responsibility to turn it into significance. Success can be about ourselves, and that is perfectly acceptable. Significance is when it becomes about others. As Bob Buford says in his book, *Halftime*,[20] "If the first half was a quest for success, the second half is a journey to significance." I wish you nothing but health, wealth, and happiness. Go have fun, stick together, and play like a champion.

JAKE

ABOUT THE AUTHOR

Jake Dixon is the Founder and CEO of The Locker Room Real Estate Coach & Training organization that specializes in partnering with broker owners and their agents to increase growth, retention, productivity, and profitability. The Locker Room began in 2016 when Jake was one of the Top Productivity Coaches in the country. Jake was selected by AgentFire as one of the Top 50 Real Estate Coaches and served on the SUCCESS Coaching Founder's Circle. Jake was also named a Top Real Estate Coach by COACH Foundation and a Top 25 Real Estate Trendsetter by *SUCCESS*® magazine.

Jake and his team have served hundreds of brokerages and tens of thousands of agents. Jake graduated from the University of North Florida where he played college baseball and proceeded to play professional baseball within the Anaheim Angels organization, which has served as inspiration when developing The Locker Room. He is also co-founder of the TLR Leadership & Coaching Academy and Founder of The Champion's Network. In his spare time, Jake loves spending time with his wife and two daughters, playing with his dogs, traveling, speaking, and even searching for Native American Artifacts to add to his collection.

Jake-Dixon.com

CONNECT WITH JAKE

Facebook: @CannonballBook
Instagram: @CoachJakeDixon
Company Website: TLRNation.com
Speaker Page: TLRNation.com/jake-dixon
The Champion's Network: MyChampionsNetwork.com
TLR Leadership & Coaching Academy Facebook:
@TLRNationAcademy
The Locker Room Facebook: @LockerRoomCoaching
The Locker Room Instagram: @TLRNationCoaching

ENDNOTES

1   "Willpower Definition & Meaning." *Merriam-Webster*, Merriam-Webster, www.merriam-webster.com/dictionary/willpower.

2   Sinek, Simon. *Start with Why: How Great Leaders Inspire Everyone to Take Action.* Penguin Books Ltd, 2011.

3   Covey, Stephen R. *The Seven Habits of Highly Effective People: Restoring the Character Ethic: 7 Habits of Highly Effective People.* Simon & Schuster, 1989.

4   Nightingale, Earl. *Earl Nightingale's the Strangest Secret.* Gardners Books, 2007, *Audible*, https://www.audible.com/pd/The-Strangest-Secret-and-This-I-Believe-Audiobook/B00OAMMWJQ.

5   Andrews, Andy, et al. *The Traveler's Gift: Seven Decisions That Determine Personal Success ; Mastering the Seven Decisions That Determine Personal Success: An Owner's Manual to the New York Times Bestseller the Traveler's Gift.* Thomas Nelson Publishers, 2008.

6   Ibid.

7   Berger, Warren. *A More Beautiful Question: The Power of Inquiry to Spark Breakthrough Ideas.* Langara College, 2019.

8   Willink, Jocko, and Leif Babin. *Extreme Ownership: How U.S. Navy Seals Lead and Win.* Macmillan, 2018.

9   Andrews, Andy, et al. *The Traveler's Gift: Seven Decisions That Determine Personal Success ; Mastering the Seven Decisions That Determine Personal Success: An Owner's Manual to the New York Times Bestseller the Traveler's Gift.* Thomas Nelson Publishers, 2008.

10   Kim, W. Chan, and Renée Mauborgne. *Blue Ocean Strategy: How to Create Uncontested Market Space and Make the Competition Irrelevant.* Harvard Bus Review Press, 2016.

11   "Four Stages of Competence." *Wikipedia*, Wikimedia Foundation, 1 Feb. 2024, en.wikipedia.org/wiki/Four_stages_of_competence.

12   Maxwell, John C. *Sometimes You Win - Sometimes You Learn: Life's Greatest Lessons Are Gained from Our Losses.* Center Street, 2015.

13   Messer, Andrea. "Linguistics May Be Clue to Emotions, According to Penn State Research." *Penn State University*, Penn State News, www.psu.edu/news/research/story/linguistics-may-be-clue-emotions-according-penn-state-research/.

14   Ibid.

15   Zemeckis, Robert, director. *Forrest Gump*. Paramount Pictures, 1994.

16   Kosinski, Joseph, director. *Top Gun*. Paramount Pictures, 1986.

17   Sheils, Jim, et al. *The Family Board Meeting: You Have 18 Summers to Create Lasting Connection with Your Children.* Ethos Collective, 2023, *Audible,* https://www.audible.com/pd/The-Family-Board-Meeting-You-Have-18-Summers-to-Create-Lasting-Connection-with-Your-Children-Audiobook/B07GVQTCXL.

18   Andrews, Andy, et al. *The Traveler's Gift: Seven Decisions That Determine Personal Success ; Mastering the Seven Decisions That Determine Personal Success: An Owner's Manual to the New York Times Bestseller the Traveler's Gift.* Thomas Nelson Publishers, 2008.

19   Alessandra, Anthony J., and Michael J. O'Connor. *The Platinum Rule: Discover the Four Basic Business Personalities--and How They Can Lead You to Success*. Warner Books, 1998.

20   Buford, Bob P. *Halftime*. Zondervan, 2016.

Made in the USA
Monee, IL
13 June 2024

59359477R00134